THE
DORKING REVIEW

THE DORKING REVIEW

WRITTEN BY:

Iain Benson
Lynton Cox
Robert J Halls
Gary Hoadley
Stuart Kerr
Stuart Mitchell
Gary Moore
Peter Oliver
Neil Scott
Sarah Steinbach
Ian Youngs

EDITED BY:

Gary Moore

ILLUSTRATED BY:

Robert J Halls

Editor's note.

Nice place Dorking. It's got a very well laid out pay and display car park, and a particularly exciting dry-cleaners located just off of the main shopping area. Residents and visitors alike can also pass a most agreeable summer's afternoon admiring the town's extensive collection of street lights and public litter bins.

However, during the winter, when the cold easterly wind blows in from across the vast empty expanse of the plastics factory's car park next to the B2347, it can be a different story; the good people of Dorking are then obliged to seek shelter indoors.

It is during those long dark winter nights that The Dorking Review comes into its own, as not only do the articles within give the reader a warm comforting glow, but they can also chuck it on the fire once they've read it.

This edition of The Dorking Review contains all of the good things that the discerning reader would expect from a book, including a lot of words – some of which are arranged into coherent sentences, a few pictures, and a free DNA sample from someone who once visited Ipswich.

All of the really good bits were written by someone else, and all of the mistakes are naturally my own.

Gary Moore.

THE
DORKING REVIEW

A

COMPLETE TISSUE

OF

LIES

CHARGING RAM BOOKS
TORONTO

Charging Ram Books
& e-books
An imprint of 2204112 Ontario Inc., Toronto
may be ordered through booksellers or by contacting:

www.ChargingRam.com.

September 11, 2011

FIRST EDITION

ISBN: 978-0-9877452-0-0 - English softcover

Library and Archives Canada – Bibliothèque et Archives Canada
www.collectionscanada.gc.ca

NEWS

SCHIZOPHRENIC BURGLAR ARRESTS HIMSELF

A burglar, who shares his split personality with a high ranking police officer, yesterday shocked the local constabulary when he arrested himself and brought himself in for questioning at the local police station.

"Thirty years on the force, and I've never seen anything like this before," Desk sergeant Bobby Copper told our reporter. "He came into the station trying to push his own arm up his back, shouting that he was innocent and then in the same breath telling himself he was nicked."

Bewildered policemen escorted Frank Knutt to a detention cell, where he interviewed himself and took a statement before demanding to be thrown into a proper cell and given a bit of a kicking.

Knutt admitted to himself that he'd broken into a furniture store and tried to steal a Welsh dresser and a chest of drawers, before disturbing himself and placing himself under arrest. It was lucky for him that he happened to be present when the burglary took place and that by swiftly intervening with himself he was able to prevent himself from making off with the stolen goods.

Knutt is expected to appear before the town magistrate accused of burglary and police brutality. It is thought that he will appeal for the maximum sentence with time off for good behaviour and easy access to a police car with flashing lights and a siren.

Skoob 1999

MARY POPPINS HELD ON DRUG CHARGES

Mary Poppins, the famous nanny, was once again being held at Paddington Green police station on suspicion of possession of illegal drugs, with intent to supply.

Poppins, 82, who was immortalised in the 1964 film Mary Poppins, as portrayed by Julie Andrews, is suspected of supplying hallucinogenic drugs to minors in her care in order to keep them in good order.

A concerned parent we spoke to told us: "She was always a bit weird, and when she handed the kids back, they always seemed kind of spaced out. They'd talk about stuff like cartoons being real and drinking tea on the ceiling, and then they'd start singing these really off the wall songs. This woman is evil. They ought to lock her up and throw the door away."

A friend of Poppins, Bert the chimney sweep, is heading up a 'Free Mary Poppins' campaign. Bert, immortalised by Dick Van Dyke's portrayal of him in the 1964 film, told us: "She's blinkin' well innocent. Everybody knows that. I mean, cor blimey luv a duck and bless 'er little cotton socks, she ain't no blinking drug dealer, and she sure as eggs are eggs wouldn't give acid or skunk or any of that malarkey to the blinkin' nippers. Be more than 'er gor blimey job's worth.

Innit. She's been me blinkin' mate for years and I chooses me mates like I chooses me brush bristles with great bloomin' care. Chim chim cheroo, supercalifragilisticexpialidocious, spoonful of sugar 'elps the methadone go down and that, mate. Innocent's wot she is I tells yer, an' no mistake."

Poppins, who has previously been convicted on drug related charges, has spent several sojourns in HMP Holloway, where she is known to fellow inmates as Queenie. She is believed to have run B Wing, from her cell with an iron fist.

Skoob 1999

MAN ENTERED FOR CRUFTS DECLARED BARKING

Bob Pomeroy, who entered this year's Crufts as a wolfhound, has been declared barking mad under the 1864 Mad Dog Act.

Dorking Magistrates heard today how Pomeroy, a 56 year old supermarket manager from Leatherhead, entered Crufts as a 7 year old wolfhound 'Beau Bob' in the Working Gundog section of this year's competition.

"I immediately suspected Beau Bob was not a wolfhound," explained legendary 68 year old judge, Dora Cattermole.
"For a start, he didn't appear to be comfortable on all fours. Then, when I asked his handler, Mr Mundy, why Beau Bob's tail had been removed, he simply told me I'd have to ask the dog. Finally, when I had my customary feel between Beau Bob's back legs, he got far more excited than any wolfhound I've come across in 30 years as a circuit judge."

Eye witnesses revealed that it took six male judges to drag Beau Bob off Dora Cattermole and into a ringside cage.
"The dog had a paw up Dora's tartan skirt and was foaming at the mouth," declared ironmonger and poodle connoisseur Vernon Moult.
"Passing sentence, Chairman of the bench Roy Figgis growled, "This tailless wolfhound, Beau Bob, is a disgrace to Crufts name and reputation."

Seconds later, muzzled Bob Pomeroy, wearing a smart two-piece suit and red tie, was led away for further training at Her Majesty's pleasure.

84 year old chihuahua, Vic Noblet from Kettering, won best in show.

Juanita Juan

ALCOHOLISM 'HALVED AT A STROKE' AS PUB CHAIN INTRODUCE 3-D BEER GOGGLES

Public house giant J.D.Witherfork today rolled out a revolutionary hi-tech accessory for customers, which in trials has produced a 50% cut in incidents of drunkenness throughout their establishments.

"Think of them as hi-tech rose-tinted glasses," beamed CEO Jimmy Witherfork at the press launch of the device in flagship public house 'The Slug and Pickled Walnut', Dorking.

"These 3D Beer Goggles enable the wearer to spend an evening in the pub surveying customers and bar staff in an amorous way, without having to be fuelled by copious amounts of alcohol. We estimate that the effect of the goggles is equivalent to drinking 5 pints of lager."

"The benefit to the wearer is enormous. They can engage in coherent conversation with the object(s) of their desire, flirting and even 'pulling' them without the deleterious effects of intoxication – reeking of booze, slobbering and slurring of words, involuntary farting, incontinence and being incapable of uttering anything more cogent than 'You're lovely, you are'." he says.

"The devices fit tightly around the wearers head – they need to be goggles rather than glasses," he adds, "so that they don't accidentally get knocked off during the evening. The shock of returning to reality could be traumatic, not to mention, immensely embarrassing. We intend to lease them out for 24 hours so that the awful early next morning realisation on waking up to the actuality of what has occurred *and* what their pick-up *really* looks like is eliminated. And no headache!" he enthuses.

Witherfork seems unconcerned with the possible downside for his business the goggles could produce; profits from sales of alcoholic drinks may plummet accordingly by 50%.

"We figure that customers will look at the positive benefits, primarily their 'leg-over' success ratio that the goggles will bring, and consequently be prepared to pay a premium price for them. This will more than make up for the drink sales downturn. That," he winks, "and the fact that we already charge them through the nose for fizzy lemonade and water. It's win-win for all concerned!"

pinxit

AID FOR WELSH DYSLEXICS REFUSED – MORE RAIDING PARTIES EXPECTED ALONG BORDER

An appeal from the Welsh Assembly for help to support the fight against dyslexia in the Land of Song has been refused by UNESCO.

Spokesman for UNESCO Giancarlo Frillipanti said that there are many worthy causes around the world to which his organisation lends its aid but they require a certain effort to be made by the countries involved before providing funding. Self-help is the key and Wales has so far either done nothing, or taken the self-help route to criminal extremes and thus the decision must be no, again.

He continued: "The Welsh have for many years insisted in using a language devoid of vowels, any sensible spelling or pronunciation, so what can they expect?"

Although some progress has been made; and he cited the example of the years of work that went into perfecting Cardiff and Swansea from the original Caerdydd and Abertawe.

"But," he added, "how anyone could ever have reached those levels of stupid spelling in the first place, God only knows."

"However," he continued, "there is still much progress to be made. They have still done nothing about Bettws Y Coed, which turns a perfectly respectable town into a somewhat amibiguous place, and about which we advised them after their first failed application. Do they mean Betty's Coeducational School or what?"

"They made an utter mess of Llanfairpwllgwygyllgogery-chwyrndropwilllllantisiliogogogoch, having stolen vowels from the English during raiding parties across Offa's Dyke, and just sticking them anywhere. Did they think we wouldn't notice? The poor people of Shrewsbury, whose original 'o' went into 'Ruabon' had to cadge an 'e' from Ellesmeere in Cheshire. This was only because they could spare one without a radical pronunciation change."

"O's have been severely depleted in bordering counties as a result, and it is feared that they might have to be reintroduced from Woomera and Calgoorie in Australia (where they can be replaced by U and B respectively) to prevent complete extinction in the area. The people of Wollagong generously volunteered one of theirs but that would have been too much of a sacrifice to accept."

"There is a perfectly civilised country next door, with a whole Commonwealth of Nations ready and willing to help, but the Welsh steadfastly refuse to have anything to do with them, instead, making warlike gestures and entering into cross-border toponymic skirmishes. Closing the pubs on Sundays did help reduce drunken incursions, however, there is evidence that these are beginning again. If this continues it will be necessary for UN peacekeepers to be sent in."

A spokesman for the Welsh Assembly said: "Yw cwn bggr yff, yw pwny lttll ynglwsh brstds nd gw stch ywr hydd wp ywr rs yff yw thynch wyr gwyn tw yws ywr fwchn vawills!"

Lunchtime O'Bookcase, cultural correspondant.

LC

MAN SURVIVES YO-YO SUICIDE ATTEMPT

Clifton Suspension Bridge, Bristol – Sightseers at Brunel's landmark bridge over the Avon Gorge were stunned when a man calmly stood in front of them and tossed himself off.

"I saw this guy walking along with a huge coil of rope under his arm. He tied one end to a strut in the middle of the bridge, noosed the other end round his neck and just jumped!" said one horrified eyewitness. "He was plunging feet first. That's when we saw that there was a ship passing underneath!"

The man plunged almost the entire 245-ft drop when, to the amazement of onlookers, he hit the ship and suddenly shot back up towards the bridge. According to another tourist, "He was like a human yo-yo! Up down, up down...bonking himself on the bottom of the bridge, falling back down to the ship and zinging back up again. Everyone's heads were going up and down following him, like spectators at a vertical tennis match. It'd have been hilarious...if it wasn't so tragic."

Eventually, the man, named by police as Kenneth Armstrong, was rescued by the crew aboard the merchant ship, which had a cargo of bouncy castles on the deck. Police said that he had earlier broken into a nearby shed owned by an Xtreme sports club and unwittingly stolen a bunjee rope.

He was taken to Bristol General Infirmary with bruises and a sore throat. A hospital spokesman described Armstrong's condition as 'stretchy'.

pinxit

INTERNET CRASHES AS SPINNING BALLERINA THROWS UP

The Internet was plunged into darkness today seconds after millions of computer users around the world witnessed the ubiquitous whirling ballerina on website advertisements begin to vomit violently.

"It went everywhere. Real projectile pukey stuff, flying off the ad's picture frame and onto the rest of the web-page...but SHE KEPT ON SPINNING!" said PC user Wendy van Klomp, an estate agent from Bury. "It started me dry-retching. That's when all the screens went black."

The same story emerges around the world as thousands of computer users have been admitted to A&E with nausea and shock. The internet has now been restored, but what actually caused the crash is still a mystery.

The pirouetting dancer, Lindy Lucie, 24, who appears nude in silhouette on the webcam advert, was admitted to a central London hospital for medical investigation. A friend said that she must be 'knackered', as Ms Lucie had held down the spinning job for over six months and had performed her act for the camera 24/7 without a break, from a small Soho studio in London.

A hospital spokesman said that doctors were perplexed by Ms

Lucie's condition. "Her nausea is easing, but her leg, which she complains is in 'agony', is a source of concern. However, we've no idea which leg to treat as it seems that sometimes she's been turning on her right leg, sometimes on the left. It's bizarre.

Her condition is described as 'dizzy'.

pinxit

ACTOR'S UNION TO STRIKE OVER INTERNET'S SPINNING BALLERINA

Following yesterday's shocking incident when Lindy Lucie, globally famous for being the naked and silhouetted 'Spinning Ballerina', crashed the internet as she began projectile vomiting over website pages throughout the world; performer's union Equity have now balloted to strike over her work conditions.

"The way Lindy has been treated is positively inhumane," said leading actor Simon Callous. "Pirouetting non-stop in the nude for days at a time- and on one leg and then having to give a little hop! No wonder she puked her ring like that. I'd have demanded at least a tutu. Er... if I were a girl, that is. It's sheer exploitation."

Ms Lucie, 24, has now been released from hospital and was back rehearsing her unique naked pirouette in the dimly lit Soho webcam studio of 'internet entrepreneur' Mark Suckersburgh.

When questioned about the inhumanity of Ms Lucie having to constantly spin for hours on one leg, Mr Suckerburgh countered, a twinkle in his heavily bagged eyes: "One leg? Yes it's hard work, although it really does depend on which way you look at it."

"We've also hired Lindy's pet rabbit for another web advert for the same client." He enthused. "Her rabbit, when turned and vibrated sideways looks like a duck! It's amazing – and it's pulling in a lot of 'hits' money for Lindy."

Ms Lucie, who is currently in between rehearsals for her slightly amended routine which apparently will involve a pole, refused to answer most questions from the assembled press throng, but she did respond to one. When asked about her versatile vibrating rabbit, Ms Lucie glared angrily at the questioner and said: "how did you know about that? That's an extremely personal and hurtful question. Particularly as the batteries are flat – it's as useful as a chocolate teapot at the moment."

The first strike of Equity's members is expected to occur during tonight's revival of 'Oh Calcutta', in the infamous scene when all male actors on stage strip off and appear naked. One of them was quoted as saying: "That's when we all down tools."

pinxit

DOUBLE-BARREL MADNESS MUST STOP SAY REGISTRARS

Tired of endless double-barrelled surnames, UK registrars have called for common sense to prevail.

A recent trend for both partners in a marriage to keep their family names and put them together is causing complications in the registrar's record keeping.

Said Petula Blender, chief Registrar at a posh London borough:
"You have the situation these days where a young lady is reluctant to give up her maiden name, so she and her hubby put their names together. It also gives them something of a *faux* high-class gloss, doesn't it?

So newlyweds Mr and Mrs Probate-Clunderbunk have a couple of little ones themselves. Little Billy Probate-Clunderbunk grows up and wants to marry Mary Froodle-Torpedo.

Mary is so proud of her parent's moniker that the story is repeated and we get a Mr and Mrs Probate-Clunderbunk-Froodle-Torpedo.

What happens when Mr and Mrs Probate-Clunderbunk-Froodle-Torpedo's little girl grows up and falls in love with Damien Locksmith-Menwith-Postulate-Blute?

I'll tell you... we have a next generation saddled with Probate-Clunderbunk-Froodle-Torpedo-Locksmith-Menwith-Postulate-Blute. And so it goes on *ad-nauseum* until it takes several hours just to read the names out in the ceremony and registrars everywhere suffer from permanent writer's cramp.

Where will it end, I ask you?"

SM

MAN WITH THREE BUTTOCKS DENIES HAVING AN ADVANTAGE IN ARSE KICKING COMPETITION.

This year's district games were once again held at the Sir Oswald Mosely Memorial playing fields and the fine weather helped to attract a record number of visitors. Alongside the staging of all of the traditional local sports, there was also more trade stalls and side shows than ever before, including those of Mick's Spliffs, The Department of Health and Social Security, Legal Aid Solicitors, The massed ghetto-blasters of the Fair-Fields social housing scheme and The Thames Valley Police Mobile Surveillance unit.

The opening ceremony saw a thirty minute spectacular by the Belgian National projectile vomiting display team, which was very well received, and was rewarded with a sustained round of applause by all those that witnessed it.

The games themselves commenced with the Self-Induced Face-Lift Event, which was won by local girl Nikki Brown, who picked up first place having wound a standard packet of hair bobbles around her pony tail to a staggering tension of 15 Mega-Joules, equivalent to the effect of hanging a mark two Vauxhall Astra from her hair.

As always the tattoo section was very popular, with Wayne Atlee walking away with the prize for "Best Spelt Home-made Tattoo" His winning limb featuring the names of his eight children with only two minor spelling errors, - A remarkable achievement indeed! His current girlfriend, Wanda Gaitskill made it a family double when she took first place in the art section with the full length tattoo on her back of the legendary Woolworths Shop-Lifting raid of 1994 during which over 50% of the store's stock was removed in a single afternoon.

The "most inappropriate use of the national flag" event was a close fought competition which was finally secured by Mrs Vera Palmerston with her customised colostomy bag. She had been close run by Brian Heath who had entered his bell-end on which he had drawn the flag using a biro. Unfortunately during the judging, Mr Heath was unable to contain his excitement, resulting in the flag being displayed upside-down thus leading to his disqualification.

There was some dispute when Lance Wilson was accused of having an unfair advantage in the individual arse kicking competition due to his naturally occurring third buttock. Mr Wilson vigorously denied that it gave him any advantage and a heated dispute took place. In the event, it mattered not as the prize was taken by visiting American; Troy "Kick-ass" Bush, who managed to kick himself with such force that he required admittance to the district hospital for treatment. Local honour was restored by Mrs Bev Thatcher in the doubles event when she gained a new games record by punting her husband an impressive eight feet, ten inches with a single well aimed swing of her Reebok.

In the minor events, John Baldwin took first place in the "Largest roll of fat on the back of the neck" competition. Andy MacMillan won the "Inappropriate remark to the wife's sister" event, and Winston Salisbury secured the "Undetected borrowing of ten pounds from the girlfriend's purse" race.

The games wound up in fine style with the traditional race to cash-converters with the neighbour's TV followed by the spending of the proceeds in The White Lion. All in all a most enjoyable afternoon for the district's dysfunctional extended families. The event is scheduled to take place again next year providing that the local council can clear up the mess left by this year's event in time.

GM

DORKING BRIT LAUNCHED INTO SPACE ON STAIRLIFT

Barely 50 years after the USSR and USA first put a human into space, the UK yesterday, finally achieved the same giant leap in rocket technology – when 97 year old Edith Pickles became the first British astronaut put into permanent orbit by a wholly British designed, built and owned vehicle.

"As far as we can ascertain, Mrs Pickles was on her stairlift when a gas explosion occurred in her house in Dorking," said Astrophysicist Professor Hans Niesanbumzy-Dayzie. "A heady cocktail of the original gas explosion and the butane propellent supply under her seat – plus a powerful biochemical cocktail in Mrs Pickles' colostomy and urinary incontinence bags have somehow unleashed an enormous propulsion effect which accelerated her to the 18,000 mph needed to escape the earth's gravity."

"It was like that scene from the end of Charlie and the Chocolate Factory," said one eyewitness to the impromptu launch. "There was a huge explosion and 'Whoosh', she went straight through the roof in her chair and shot up into the sky like a bullet."

Dr Helen Sharman, first Briton in space aboard a Soviet Soyuz in 1991, was full of admiration for the plucky Mrs Pickles. "Amazing. Edith had the "Right Stuff" from the sounds of it. The 'stuff' being an explosive mix thousands of times more powerful than conventional Lox (rocket fuel)."

The national press have already named the British space-craft 'Brown Streak' with tributes pouring in from around the world hailing the intrepid spirit of the senior citizen.

The Minister for Technology issued this statement:
"Yet again we see the strength of British expertise and private enterprise come to the fore. It's one small step for a stairlift, one giant Stairway to Heaven. Edith, we salute you. Wherever you are."

Amateur astronomers with medium sized telescopes in the South of England will be able to see Mrs Pickles and 'Brown Streak' in the Western skies, close to Uranus transit and Cassiopea, tomorrow night at 23:47 GMT.

pinxit

BIRDMAN OF DORKING
DIES ON MAIDEN FLIGHT

Human bird Bob Pomfroy is dead!

He took-off from the summit of Box Hill at 8:15 am today, but his body was discovered an hour later in light undergrowth beside the A25, midway between Dorking and Guildford.

Locally born and bred, 56 year old Pomfroy made headlines in January, when he had 10,000 bird feathers implanted into his skin.

"At Bob's request, I turned him into the world's first flying ostrich," explained consultant surgeon Professor Arthur Mouton-Birdbath.

Pomfroy, a local ferret breeder and authority on suburban pigeons, believed humans would be capable of sustained flight, if only they had feathers.

"He spent fifteen years studying dead starlings at our dining-room table," wept his distraught wife Marlene. "Calculating what he called 'the precise mechanics of flight'. In the end he claimed he knew exactly how many feathers per square inch he would need. By Christmas there was nothing Bob didn't know about being a bird," she said. "So we decided to go ahead with the operation. As I told Professor Birdbath. To most people my husband is a boring ferret breeder. Now make him the kind of man everyone will look up to."

Thousands turned out to see Bob Pomfroy take to the sky.

"We were standing two hundred feet below, ready to rush him straight to hospital," said elderly paramedic Ted Warnock. "The moment the band started playing the Dam Busters march, we started the motor of the ambulance. As Mr Pomfroy prepared for take-off, we had six of us waiting with an outstretched blanket. And a stretcher in case we missed him."

The great moment had arrived. Pomfroy slowly squatted down, bending his knees. Eyes wide open and looking straight ahead, he took a deep breath. Then with both arms flapping wildly, he leapt off the edge, and out into the freedom of the open sky.

To the amazement of everyone, ghoulishly gathered to witness a man plunge to his certain death, the local ambulance service turned out to be surplus to requirements.

"He went off like a startled crow," said disappointed bystander Reg Pillock. "Straight as an arrow, and higher and higher into the sky, until he vanished into a passing cloud. Nobody clapped. We just stood there with our mouths wide open. Struck dumb. Gob-smacked by the sight of a middle aged man flying into the distance. He had a smile on his face like he was some kind of bird, without a care in the entire world."

Forty five minutes later, pig-breeder Len Normington was carefully driving his massive 68 ton lorry along the M25, midway between Dorking and Guildford.

"I was heading to market. Peacefully finishing me ham and cheddar sandwich with mustard and pickle, when suddenly I saw this crazy ostrich heading in my direction," explained shocked Mr Normington ten minutes later. "I ask you! A bloody great ostrich! Diving straight down towards me. Slap into me windscreen. Stupid bloody bird. Never stood a chance."

Juanita Juan

LARGE HADRON COLLIDER SUCCESS DOWN TO LOCAL SPARKY

Egg heads operating the Large Hadron Collider (LHC) have local electrician Dave Coaxial to thank for their successes over recent weeks.

The collider, which is operated by the European Organisation for Nuclear Research (CERN), is in a huge circular tunnel between France and Switzerland near Geneva.

Over recent weeks, boffins operating the LHC have succeeded in creating conditions similar to those which existed just seconds after the 'Big Bang'. They also claim to have captured anti-matter atoms.
    But they would have been nowhere without Dave.

He told us: "Me and the missus, Karen, well we were having a city break in Geneva and were in this bar having a drink one night when we got talking to this guy.
    He told us he worked at this LHC thing, but they were having problems – it wasn't working. I told him I was a sparky, and asked him if he wanted me to have a look at it for them. Well, he said that would be great. So he took me there the next day and I gave the systems a once-over and saw the problem at once – they'd blown a 13 amp fuse in one of the computer's power plugs. I normally charge £250 just for the call out, but when I told the guys they could have this one for free they bought Karen and me lunch. Nice one."

SM

'FLASH-FART' SENSORS INSTALLED BY DORKING POLICE

After an abnormally high number of gang-related incidents involving spontaneous combustion, Dorking constabulary have installed equipment from the US to detect flatulent outbursts.

"Incidents of youth gang drive-by 'Flash-Farts', where highly volatile buttock emissions are deliberately set alight to torch passers-by, are dramatically on the increase," says chief Supt Chris Bean. "It has become the weapon of choice in local gang vendettas."

It is the first time the Grosshammer Ultrawave Flatulence Finder (GUFF) System – which can pick up flatulent emissions within a 25m (82ft) radius, has been deployed in the UK.

Dorking Police said the sensors had been placed high up on buildings in the south-central part of the town known as the 'Balti Triangle'. The area with the highest concentration of Balti and Curry houses in Surrey.

"Gang members deliberately go on vindaloo blow-outs, washing it down with copious amounts of highly gassed lagers," explains Bean. "It's not only extremely dangerous to their victims but – with the very real possibility of flaming blowback – potentially lethal to the perpetrator."

The new system records an audio clip and sends police a GPS location. It can tell if multiple emissions were expelled, whether they came from a stationary or moving location, the number of anuses involved and in which order they were 'pumped' and has an 85% accuracy rate.

"If the offending raspers are committed indoors, or with a silencer - SBDs (Silent But Deadly) as we call them – then the GUFF system is, understandably, not so effective. Those expelled outside have the best chance of being detected," says CS Bean.

However, Local Residents' Association spokesman Ron Sneed voiced reservations about the experiment. "We all want 'Flash-Farting' off our streets, but are worried that innocent bystanders like my Gran, who has problems with her tum, may be targeted by police squads smashing down her door every time she drops a bundle owing to follow-through."

'Operation Thunderpants' will be active in Dorking from next Thursday.

pinxit

TOBOGGANISTS TO BE RELEASED INTO THE WILD

The Ministry of Agriculture, Fisheries and Food has announced that Tobogganists are once more to be allowed to freely roam the countryside, following one of the longest recorded periods of incarceration of a minority group.

It has been over 30 years since the native British Tobogganist has been seen in the wild, following their enforced imprisonment under the 'Dangerous Sportsman Act' of 1978. Since that time, all British Tobogganists have been held in the government's secure compound on the outskirts of the unattractive town of Grantham in Lincolnshire; the site having been specially chosen for its low ceilinged accommodation and insipid views of a landscape that is not only mind numbingly dreary, but also as flat as 'a witch's tit'. Within that secure site, specialists have managed to change the once widely feared British Tobogganist from what was an adrenaline-fuelled, unemployable, aristocratic lunatic to what is now claimed to be a reasonably law abiding (if still somewhat unintelligent) person. This dramatic turnaround is claimed to have been achieved by the use of selective breeding and controlled aversion therapy.

Not everyone however is happy with the announcement, and there have been worries that the chaos of the past; culminating in a catastrophe such as the British bob-sleigh disaster during the Helsinki Winter Olympics may once more repeat itself.

Pip Emma – Head of the National Tobogganist Re-Alinement Centre who has worked with gradient related sports offenders for the past ten years was eager to allay the public's fears. "Tobogganists are no longer a threat to society," she said, "I can assure everyone that when the Tobogganists are released, they will continue to be under strict supervision. They understand that they are not allowed outside of Lincolnshire and they know that if they are found in possession of a tin tray or an old car bonnet they will forfeit their right to freedom."

She conceded that although it would be impossible to prevent the newly released Tobogganists from gravitating towards areas of slightly sloping ground, she believed that all reasonable measures have been taken to prevent wayward Tobogganists from lapsing into their old ways, including the banning of woolly hats and brightly coloured ski jackets within the county, and the electrifying of all the slides in the kiddies play areas.

GM

DORKING MAN WALKING PET SNAKE CAUSES TRAFFIC CHAOS

Bernard Barnowl caused the world's longest traffic jam today when he put a lead on his pet python, Monty, and took him for a walk down the A24.

Forty-two-foot reticulated python, Monty, is used to being taken for a constitutional along the lamp posts and woodland pathways on the verges of the main road.

"Daily walkies are a vital part of Monty's lifestyle," explained 48 year old milkman Barnowl. "He gets to stretch himself out, eat the odd lamb or hedgehog, have a sniff round the undergrowth and crucially mark-out his territory. Pythons are very much like dogs you know."

Things went wrong this morning when Barnowl decided to escort Monty across the road.

"I waited for a long gap in the traffic, then led him across the A24," explained Barnowl.

"I'd just reached the other side, when the stupid snake decided he wanted the loo."

"So I shouted at him. I told him straight. I said, look here Monty, your head is on one side of the A24 and your tail's on the other. This is neither the time nor place to go poo poo."

"Would he listen? No way. He just looked up like I was a complete idiot – and began the lengthy process of doing his number twos. Pythons are like that, you know, obstinate buggers."

Thankfully the drivers of the first vehicles to approach the scene were paying attention.

"As I looked ahead, I immediately noticed there was a big python stretched across the road having a crap," revealed 53 year old delivery driver Ron Huggett. "So I pulled up and waited for it to finish."

District nurse, Minnie Hardacre, did exactly the same from the opposite direction. "I know global warming's a problem. But I didn't expect pythons in Surrey quite so soon," she said.

Within an hour traffic was at a standstill all the way down to Worthing. Whilst the nearby M25 was at a halt from Heathrow right across Surrey and Kent as far as the Dartford tunnel.

"It's the worst traffic jam in history," declared Chief Inspector Bob Ballard of Surrey police. "Sixty five miles of cars and lorries all bumper to bumper."

Bloody pythons!

Juanita Juan

DORKING ARCHDEACON
MISSING IN WI 'WITCHCRAFT ORGY'

Police investigating the mysterious disappearance of a senior member of the clergy say that 'dark forces', including the Dorking Women's Institute, may be involved.

Police remain tight-lipped over the mysterious disappearance of senior clergyman Bishop Rohan Walliams. But one Dorking resident, husband of one of the WI members detained by police for questioning, has spoken out publicly on the mystery that is miring the town in scandal.

Retired ex-army Major Ian Sworter's revealing verbatim interview below offers a tantalising glimpse into a murky and sordid 'underworld' that is far from the traditional image of the Women's Institute as being merely 'Jam and Jerusalem'.

"The old Sworter constitution turns to quivering blancmange when I think of what may have happened to that young Bishop cove, as this is not the first time the male 'chosen one' has seemingly vanished off the face of the earth."

"Only two years ago, Archdeacon Rumbelow was invited to their Walpurgis meet, ostensibly to judge their 'Unusually-shaped Vegetables and Exotic Puddings Competition'. Apparently he made the tragic mistake of choosing Sidone Quate-Blanchett's Marrow

Spotted Dick over the Memsahib's Rhubarb & Cucumber Crumble. Vanished off the face of the earth, poor chap."

At this point he leant forward from his armchair and barely whispered these words, "But...last year the Constabulary found his mitre, soiled boxer shorts and a pickled walnut buried in a ditch in Tring!"

pinxit

MET OFFICE "CRAP" ADMISSION

Britain's Meteorological Office – the Met Office – is at the centre of a storm again after it was discovered that they deliberately seek to confuse TV viewers with contradictory forecasts. The latest row comes just weeks after the organisation managed to retain their contract for broadcast forecasting with the BBC. Many insiders wanted the contract to go to a rival forecaster because, they said, the Met Office was "crap."

One of their most famous gaffes was to fail to predict the hurricane that struck the south east of the country in 1987.

Now BBC viewers are up in arms over simultaneous contradictory forecasts.

One such viewer is Sid Inkwell, of Maidstone, Kent. He told us: "Oh yes, my wife and I have been keen viewers of the weather forecast now for many years. I like to watch the bulletins in the news programmes and then switch to the text version. This morning the chappie on screen was predicting huge downpours and talking of flood warnings for tonight and tomorrow. But the map on the text version was predicting clear skies and dry weather. Well, that rather put Irene and me in a quandary. Shall we venture down to the club tonight to see our friends or not?"

An unnamed source within the Met Office admitted they operated a policy of equivocation.

"Oh yes – don't tell anyone, but we make up different forecasts for each platform. The thing is, we simply don't know what's going to happen. We're pretty crap really. It all looks very scientific, what with radar pictures and everything. But really those graphics are made by interns using pencils and crayons in the back office. If you really want to know what the weather's like, you're better off sticking your head outside."

SM

LOCAL MAN MAXES OUT FOUR CREDIT CARDS ON TV CHRISTMAS SHOPPING SPREE

Local man, Martin Shuttlecock, this morning revealed how he maxed out four credit cards whilst watching late night TV shopping channel QED.

Shuttlecock explained that he'd been enjoying some pre Christmas holiday time that he'd earned, so was having a night owl evening watching the TV, when his attention was caught, held, nailed, and his wallet trashed by the QED channel, as he discovered numerous products that he couldn't live without.

The first item which grabbed Shuttlecock's undivided attention was a clever paint pad infomercial, which demonstrated an invaluable plastic painting tool which would effectively enable him to paint the whole house in about seventeen minutes, with no drips or splashes. For only £38.99 plus p&p plus vat plus shipping, which totalled £217.98

He explained: "I knew I'd been going wrong somewhere with the painting. I was paying £3.99 for a set of paint pads, but they can't possibly have been up to the job at that price. I can't wait 'til they deliver my magical new painting tool. I might even start a business and go round painting the neighbour's houses for a small fee. I'll be quids in! Wah-hey"!

Then, just as Shuttlecock was about to turn in for the night, another infomercial came on the TV claiming to cut required wardrobe space by up to 80% - so he purchased 50 scientifically tested and guaranteed , bulk reducing coat hangers for £118.99 plus p&p.

"That works out at just over two quid a hanger"! Shuttlecock enthused. "And if that doesn't represent good value for money, then I'll be buggered if I know what does."

Shuttlecock then went on to sponsor various endangered species of wild animals, buy a mattress of the same design as the one used by astronauts when they landed on the moon, some crystal things that get really stubborn stains out of virtually anything, a daft exercise thing which was basically a cross between a dustbin lid and a roundabout, and a Chinese manufactured artificial Christmas tree with lights that catch fire at some point, with a discounted Chinese made fire extinguisher thrown in from a dealer in South Carolina, USA.

In fact Shuttlecock was just about to buy a 98 CD box set of *The Sounds of Somerset* for seventeen monthly instalments of £19.99 with a free whale song CD thrown in, when an irate and long suffering Anne Shuttlecock stormed downstairs and commanded him to get to bed immediately. And called him some choice names.

"He really is a daft bastard," sighed Anne. "God knows why I ever married the silly twat."

Skoob 1999

CHAOS AS FATHER CHRISTMAS FAILS CRB CHECK

Finland:- Shockwaves of dismay and disbelief in Lappland, certain to burgeon into avalanches of anger and disappointment in the UK, emerged today as the Criminal Records Bureau in London announced that 'after an intensive investigation by the CRB', FATHER CHRISTMAS has been denied his mandatory certification to work within 200 yards of any children under the age of 18 over the Christmas period.

"We don't normally comment on such decisions" said head of the Bureau Dr Gillian McHeath, "But I would say this to Mr Christmas – *if,* that is his real name: Before you start stumbling and fumbling around a million UK kid's bedrooms, make sure you get your story straight."

"It is unconscionable and beyond belief that an elderly male – with a dubious background history to say the least – who has a record as long as your arm for giving millions of vulnerable children 'presents', 'sweeties' and treats for being, as he himself admits 'good' – is free to continue his abhorrent practices. That, and the fact that this disgusting man admits to breaking into millions of people's homes with the express intent of heading straight to the bedrooms of innocent children to 'give them joy'...well – it doesn't bear thinking about."

"To compound these horrific crimes, Mr Christmas again freely admits to stealing sherry, whisky and other alcoholic drinks, along with assorted festive sweetmeats *from each and every house he burgles* – before getting back into his transport and driving off!"

"We've estimated that he must, on average, consume the equivalent of 175,000 bottles of whisky – in one night! Stereo-typical, if I may add, of most Finnish men – permanently drunk, F1-driving kiddie-fiddlers."

A vitriolic campaign by the British press and media protesting at the decision and its ramifications is anticipated, with online communities Twitter and FaceBook already calling for Dr McHeath to resign and 'Go f*ck herself'.

More from 'Santa's Ghetto' as Winter breaks...

pinxit

BBC RADIO 4'S 'TODAY' CAUSES LISTENER'S HEAD TO EXPLODE

A Radio 4 listener's head exploded this morning during the news programme, *Today.*

At about 6:45 am, retired journalist Mr Gethyn Parabola was drinking a cup of tea in his kitchen with the radio on.

His wife Mifanwy, said: "It has been coming for some time. Gethyn boils over every time he hears the expression 'in place' – especially when used by journalists, who, he says, should know better.

"Every single day, you hear interviewees referring to 'legislation has been *put in place*; 'new security measures are being *put in place*; the plans are *in place...*'

"He always moans about it being lazy English and that it's always in the passive voice. This morning, it was during a reading of the headlines when the reader said something about the EU loan to Ireland being 'put in place'."

Well that was it...he dropped his tea cup, sat there, rigid, and his head, well it just exploded. The doctors say he will probably be all right, but he has to stay away from TV and radio news and documentaries for a while. They also recommend keeping clear of newspapers, which seem to be just as guilty.

SM

LOCAL MAN CAUGHT UP IN TRAVEL CHAOS - CANCELLED CHRISTMAS TRAIN ALMOST CAUSES SEVERE FROSTBITE

Local man, Martin Shuttlecock, was today recovering at home following a harrowing ordeal as he prepared for the Christmas holiday from work by arranging for a colleague to drop him off at a station close to his workplace, but yet strangely out in the middle of nowhere, after his final day at work.

Expecting to catch the 19:04 train bound for Dorking, Shuttlecock purchased a train ticket from a machine and hurriedly smoked a cigarette, expecting to be whisked homeward in a very short time.

Shuttlecock recalls smiling contentedly as he heard the bray of a donkey from a frosty neighbouring field, but for this simple man, delight quickly degenerated into a feeling of abject horror, as he cast a careless glance at the electronic information board, which revealed that the train he had been expecting at 19:04 was not due to arrive until 19:58.

A delay of 54 minutes, caused by a broken down earlier train at Bursledon, left Shuttlecock in something of a dilemma. The cold was bitter, the wind cutting with the ferocity of a great white shark, and he had quite a lengthy time to endure on an isolated, unmanned station with no shelter other than some kind of bus shelter-like construction whose windows had long ago fallen victim to the slings and arrows of the outrageously fortunate local vandalry. Essentially, there was no glass, just an empty network of spiderwebbed frames.

Shuttlecock considered walking back in the direction from whence he came, where a warm hostelry would probably have welcomed his patronage, but a change in circumstance gave him pause for thought. The electronic information board changed, in order to signify that the 19:04 would actually be arriving at 19:57, and not 19:58, as originally stated. The hostelry in question was a ten to fifteen minute walk away, at a brisk clip, and the same back to catch the errant 19:04 at 19:57, leaving a sum total (on average) of about 29 minutes in the pub. Shuttlecock later explained that his decision to remain in situ was based on the fact that the lateness of the train had been reduced by a minute, so that theoretically, that time could be reduced even further.

So Shuttlecock elected to stay put, which proved to be – at the very least – a fateful decision.

As a stiff, freezing wind blew up, Shuttlecock recalled how he'd spent a night earlier in the year outside of London's Waterloo station nursing a broken thumb and a gashed eyebrow, and realised that his hands were now rapidly growing numb, and that the injured thumb was starting to throb quite painfully.

Pulling on a pair of thermally insulated gloves, Shuttlecock began to pace up and down the deserted platform, pausing only to glance around as two police cars with sirens screaming passed by the station. He reasoned that it was probably just as well that he hadn't taken the option of going to the pub after all. Maybe some of the locals had 'kicked off' over a game of pool or darts or something.

Then at 19:28, redemption seemed to appear, as a passing train sped through the station in Shuttlecock's direction of travel, but it did not stop to pick up the rapidly freezing lone potential passenger.

Shuttlecock later revealed that, with his heart bursting with hope, his thumb throbbing, and his knees freezing up arthritically; he still hoped to be able to catch a train to get him home by 20:30. At 19:40, a second train sped through the station, completely ignoring

Shuttlecock as it breezed swiftly by.

With the cold taking its toll, a desperate Shuttlecock took to pacing up and down the station platform.

Then, as the cold really started to sink into Shuttlecock's bones, came the bombshell from the electronic information board, that the 19:04 to Dorking had been cancelled, and that the next train would be the 20:04.

Shuttlecock himself takes up the story:
"I was frozen bleedin' rigid, I couldn't understand why they'd sent two trains right past me and left me freezing me knackers off in the middle of nowhere. Then a tannoy announcement reminded me that I couldn't smoke on the station. I thought, 'You can fuck right off' and promptly lit a fag up. I'm not being fucking dictated to by South-East Trains. But then the bastards – and I'm sure they did it just to spite me because they caught me on CCTV – announced that the fucking 20:04 was running seven minutes late. Then eleven minutes, then nineteen minutes... and to cap it all, some wanker came on the tannoy wishing me a merry Christmas and a prosperous new year. The cheeky fuckers! I lost it at that point and shouted 'Fuck off'! At the tannoy speaker. I don't think they heard me though. The train eventually arrived at twenty three minutes past eight, and when I got on it I was having shivering fits. I was so cold. I took me gloves off and me damaged thumb appeared to be turning black. I thought I had frostbite – honestly, I did. I eventually got home at a few minutes to nine, but it took me hours to thaw out. South-East Trains, - I've fucking shit 'em."

We were unable to contact South-East Trains for a response to Mr Shuttlecocks damning indictment, but a spokesman would probably have pointed out that it was a matter of logistics, and that a single customer at an unmanned halt in the middle of nowhere would simply have to eat shit for the greater good.

Skoob 1999

NOBEL WINNERS LOSE EXAMPLE OF WINNING MATERIAL

Physics Nobel Prize Winners Andrei Geim and Konstantin Novoselov have lost the very thing that won them the accolade.

Geim and Konstantin are the inventors of graphene – a flat sheet of carbon just one atom thick. It is extremely strong and is a good conductor of electricity.

However, as it is so thin it is virtually invisible.

Said a friend of the university boffins: "This is rather embarrassing for the lads.

Andrei told me they had the stuff just the other day. But he put it down somewhere before they went to the pub, and now they can't find it! Konstantin had the same problem a couple of weeks ago, but fortunately that time he'd propped it against the back of a chair in the lab and he tripped over it. I'm sure they'll find it. It can't have gone anywhere, unless it has qualities they haven't told us about yet!"

SM

LOCAL MAN IN HIGH STREET CHRISTMAS TAT SHOPPING TERROR!

Local man, Martin Shuttlecock was last night relaxing at home enjoying a quiet drink, following a traumatic High Street trip in search of tatty Christmas bargains, with long suffering wife Anne, loyal stepdaughter Gertrude, and two of his grandchildren, Millie and Vanilli.

Shuttlecock admitted that he had perhaps been a tad naïve in believing that the shopping trip would be brief, but as he'd had quite a few relaxing days, he claims to have been caught off balance.

The High Street trip began uneventfully at a Christmas market, where Gertrude purchased one of those really daft Swedish woolly hats with ear flaps, for Vanilli, from a market stall, which it later transpired she could have bought for a pound in the pound shop.

The shopping trip moved on to a discount clothing store, ironically, named Shuttlecock's. There was not much to be had in the way of bargains, so the Shuttlecock clan – after a browsing session which spun out for around forty minutes – proceeded to move on to the Pound Shop.

Shuttlecock admits that sometimes he doesn't mind a trip to the Pound Shop, because there are some useful purchases to be made there. Mostly for a pound. In fact, exclusively for a pound. Things like boxes of filter tips for hand rolled cigarettes, multipacks of cigarette papers, electronic lighters at five for a pound, and reading glasses for – you guessed it – a pound a pair.

Shuttlecock also revealed that he once purchased a DVD copy of *Edward D Wood's* **horrendously awful movie,** *Plan 9 From Outer Space*, at the Pound Shop. *For a pound.*

Other useful purchases at the Pound Shop include batteries for watches, remote controls, wireless computer keyboards, and mice, (the ones that you left and right click, not the squeaky type).

It appeared to be going well, until as Shuttlecock described to us:

"I was done me. I'd cast an eye over all the tat on offer, and was quite happy, and ready to go home, where I'd got a cold one waiting for me in the fridge. But Anne – oh no. She'd barely got started on the first aisle. I popped outside on three separate occasions for a smoke! I wish I'd have gone to the pub now and let her get on with it. She was there for nearly *three fucking hours!* Then we went on to another shop *that sold yet more fucking tat!* Millie and Vanilli got so pissed off with it all, that they started playing on the escalator. Of course, I told them that to do so is dangerous, but the poor souls were so bored out of their skulls, and tired and hungry by this time, that they sat by the door eating crisps."

And the highlight of the shopping trip?

"A black Christmas tree," Shuttlecock growled. "*A fucking **black** Christmas tree!* An artificial one, of course. Made in China probably – I don't know, I didn't look. So they're making Christmas trees exclusively for Goths and Twilight fans are they? Fucking stupid idea if you ask me. Black Christmas trees! **It's bollocks is that.** I just wanted to get home in case the miracle paint pads, and the magic window cleaning tool I ordered off the Shopping Channel had been delivered yet. Bastards"!

More as we get it.

Skoob 1999

LOCAL VICAR HAS 'BACK, SACK & CRACK' FOR CHARITY

A Dorking vicar, who had his back and delicate parts of his anatomy waxed to raise funds for his church, said "It really, really hurt, but it was worth it."

Reverend Richard Parsley, 28, of St Boniface's Church in Tootler's Lane, bared all at the Slug & Firkin pub on April Fool's Day, for the church's Roof Appeal.

Beautician, Roxanne Smedley of Brazzie's Beauty Salon, Dorking High Street, gave him the full 'Back, Sack and Crack' waxing. Without anaesthetic.

Pub landlady, Jo Taylor, who sponsored him for £100 laughed: "You've got to hand it to the vicar, he's got balls. But, when the wax was ripped off, he nearly lost them! His face was a picture." "I gave the vicar a stiffener before the beautician started the waxing, but from what I saw it obviously didn't work."

Reverend Parsley's wife, Lorraine said: "I couldn't bear to look, so I went outside. The screams were awful. Apart from a nasty rash and the limp, Dick's okay. The doctor says he'll be able to walk in a week or so if he continues with the antibiotics and talcum powder."

"I think I'll stick to jumping in a bath full of baked beans to raise funds from now on." said a tender Reverend Parsley, from his bed. "Unfortunately, I haven't been able to raise anything else since."

The appeal total for the church roof now stands at £1,500.

"Another £28,500 and we'll be able to start replacing the lead" said church warden Ken Bargs. "I just hope we get enough sponsorship from next month's St Boniface's Mum's Vajazzle for Jesus Competition to put some lead in the vicar's pencil as well." he giggled.

pinxit

DORKING REPORTER TO CLOSE

An announcement was made last week by Mr Gordon White, owner of Dorking's "other" newspaper - The Dorking Reporter, which has been experiencing financial problems for the last six months.

In the statement Mr White says "I regret that due to falling sales and the current trading situation, The Dorking Reporter is no longer a viable business, and as such it will cease to trade from the end of the month."

The Reporter was Dorking's oldest established newspaper, having been founded in 1804 and had been producing its journal every week without a break for the entire period of its existence. During that time it had diligently reported all of the happenings and events that took place in the local district. It has also produced some excellent journalists and one or two decent photographers.

Many local people will be saddened to see the end of the Reporter and will retain fond memories of it.

The high standard of writing and creative use of language - particularly in the local events section, bought many a smile to its readers, and it was a source of local pride that the town was fortunate enough to have a newspaper of such high quality that it rivalled (and often surpassed), the main Fleet Street broadsheets; particularly during the period May 1984 – June 1985.

It will probably be best remembered for its 1985 scoop story: *School Kitchen Accidentally Flooded"* which despite being brilliantly written by a young trainee reporter, never received the national acclaim that it deserved; Indeed many people at the time wondered why it was only featured on page 6, and not placed in a more prominent position. If I remember correctly, that week's main headline was: *Local MP Resigns.* - Which was written by the then chief reporter Marcus Campbell who inexplicably remained at the newspaper after the purge of 1986 which saw two other reporters fired – allegedly for drunkenness, although this was never actually proven. The closure of the newspaper will mean that all eight members of staff will lose their jobs and will now be forced to seek employment elsewhere, something that will prove to be very difficult for the current editor Mr M Campbell who, having been with the newspaper since 1979, probably won't be able to adapt to today's more technologically developed industry. He will also unfortunately miss out on his retirement party which would have taken place in three years time – although that may be a blessing as I doubt that many people would have attended it. Therefore his period of enforced unemployment will only be enlivened by being able to read the news as he stands in the dole queue with the rest of the unemployable, from a more vibrant newspaper than the one he presided over during its slide into obscurity and closure.

The staff of The Dorking Review send their sympathy to their fellow journalists at The Reporter and as a mark of respect will be holding a wake at Beckie's Pole Dancing Club on Saturday night.

GM

TREATMENT PLANT OPEN DAY A SUCCESS

For the first time since its opening in 1897, the Dorking sewage treatment plant was able to signal a red-letter day last Saturday 17th July. Having been temporarily closed for a complete refit to bring it up to the most modern standards of ISO15002 and the exigences of health and safety law, the reinstatement of normal function was celebrated by a public open day. As of Monday 19th, all discharge into the local river will have ceased, and it is hoped that normal bathing in the area will resume by the 26th, currents and tides permitting.

Visitors arrived in the teens, and the short queue was impatient for the gates to open dead on 11 am.

Grand Opening Ceremony

The ribbon was cut by the Lord Lieutenant of Surrey, The Rt Hon. Sir Peter St. John Kaished. The mayor of Dorking Mr. A Bull, in full Mayoral Regalia, was also officiating, accompanied by the honorary mayoress, his daughter Mrs Heffer.

The latter wore a white wide-brimmed hat from Mona's Millinery in Calf Street, decorated with a pot-pourri of spring flowers in red and blue and trimmed for the special occasion by Figgis's Fancy Fashions of Cattlemarket.

The clustered throng listened attentively as Sir Peter began with a short address (1 Little Street), followed by a lengthy speech extolling the virtues of modern water treatment and its contribution to public health. Draining his monogrammed hip flask he concluded that treatment plants have been far more important than the National Health Service in saving lives. What local historian could forget the fatal outbreaks of Sweating sickness, Cholera, Typhoid and the Dunghill fever that once ravaged Box Hill in the nineteenth century?

Lectures

The public was treated to a series of lectures. Firstly, Fred Steer, manager of the plant gave a 15 minute talk on *Sewage Treatment in a post-Modern World.*

The second on *The Operation of Septic Tanks and Anaerobic Digestors and the role of Zooglea remigera* by the technical manager Mr Bertram Hide was greeted with polite applause.

The most popular talk of the morning was Bill Bullock's talk '*Man and Boy in sewage – Very interesting things I have found on filters.'* Recounting the tales of fifty years at the works culminating with a lottery grant and an EU regional development award to set up a museum 'The Victoria and Albert Dumpatorium' in the shed at the back of the sprinkler beds.

Mrs Pen assisted on the Epidiascope.

Tea and Brownies having been served, the day finished with a guided tour of the plant, but owing to time and the small size of the museum only a lucky few were able to see the relics.

These included a Victorian Meissen teacup believed to have been flushed from Osborne House itself. Along with this, a box of prophylactic sheaths made of pig bladder, confirmed to have been sent as a hint to Prince Albert by the King of Prussia; a great believer himself in birth control. A gold tooth found in 1946 was missing, as was a wooden leg which had been sent away for restoration. Various replicas and models made from dewatered-sludge papier mache were available at reasonable prices.

Many amusing sideshows were featured to attract the clientèle. Brownies, Sausages and Fudge, all home made were on sale (special thanks to Myfanwy Rea and her husband Dai). For the kids there was the ever-popular 'find the Frenchman' and lots of smiling boys and girls dipped into the bran tub hoping to be the one to find Monsieur Lemerde. Highlight for the adults was the log-rolling competition on the sedimentation lagoon. The 'guess the weight of the chamber pot competition' had to be cancelled owing to a district wide delivery of All-Bran and ex-lax ready for the tourist season.

A wonderful time was had by all. Visiting specially for the open day were local man Mr Martin Shuttlecock and his wife Anne. He summed it up for everyone present before going homeward happy in their Charabanc:

"I didn't know there could be so much interesting stuff going on around a load of old shite."

You will agree readers, that that indeed could be a very appropriate motto for *The Dorking Review*.

(It is hoped that in the future, the Dorking Sewage Treatment Plant will be high on the list of local five-star tourist sites. If popular, the mayor has indicated that he will be pushing very hard to obtain monies for a full-scale Theme Park and Resort.)

LC

SUPERMARKET PLANS SUMMARY JUSTICE AFTER JUDGE'S CRITICISM

A major supermarket chain is planning to dispense summary justice at its Irish stores following advice from a judge irritated by shoplifting prosecutions. The judge, hearing a case against a Lithuanian man who stole a bottle of wine from a Tesburys store in Galway, said: "Why doesn't Tesburys deal with this sort of thing without calling the *Gardai?* The Irish taxpayer is paying for all of this."

Stung by the rebuke, Tesburys is considering its options.

Said a source close to the chain: "They're looking at various things. They're not sure a gallows or a guillotine in the car park would be very customer-friendly or encourage in-store footfall. However, research will show just how popular they might be, and if customers do like them, clearly this would be another aspect of the Tesburys customer experience that could be monetized. Freezers are sound-proof, so a bullet in the back of the head is a possibility. Or lethal injection in the manager's office or cool storage is another option. Of course, staff administering the justice would require special remuneration for the extra responsibilities, and management are in discussions with the unions about this."

SM

BRIT ATHLETE FINED FOR 'UNSPORTING BEHAVIOUR' AFTER IMPALING OPPONENT WITH JAVELIN

Another case of 'Sport-Rage' was dealt with today as promising 16 year old Javis Smedley was fined a week's pocket money for an incident during the Crystal Palace Athletics event last week.

"In his defence, he immediately apologised to the stricken competitor." said the GB Junior Athletics Coach Stuart Broad. "Although I'm not sure he heard it, as he was on the ground at the time, pinioned between the eyes. Our thoughts go out to his widow."

"To be fair, Jarvis is a young lad and was feeling a bit frustrated with the other chap, who kept on throwing longer distances than him. So he just 'lost it' for a minute and chucked the nearest thing to hand at the guy. It's a natural reaction. I've done it myself, granted, not with a javelin though. This is a tough sport with a keen competitive edge. It's not as if it's cricket y'know."

pinxit

JAVELIN IMPALER ATHLETE FINED AGAIN AFTER DISCUS DECAPITATION

Just one week after promising Olympic decathlon athlete Javis Smedley was fined for 'Unsporting Behaviour' after impaling another competitor with a javelin in an act of 'Sport-Rage', he has again appeared before the British Athletics Board for an incident at Gateshead yesterday.

Smedley 16, was preparing for the last throw in the discus part of the event when the two kilo projectile was seen to fly out of his hand and scythe into the neck of fellow competitor Daley Toms who, at the time was leading the competition.

Horrified witnesses gasped as the track-suited Toms, who was walking over to the next event with back turned to the discus circle was felled by the 'Fatal Frisbee'.

"We couldn't believe what we were seeing" said one bystander. "His head was completely severed and just flew off while his body kept walking. There was claret everywhere. Next thing we know, Smedley is swearing, running up to Daley's head, and booting it into the discus circle netting."

"Jarvis is gutted," said Smedley's coach Stuart Broad. "It just slipped out of the side of his fingers as he was practising his turning action. As soon as he realised what happened he ran over to apologise, but stumbled and accidentally kicked Daley's head into the net and then onto the running track."

The GB coach went on to pay tribute to Toms, "It must be a bit of a set back to the lad, his coach and next of kin. It's a nasty injury, but was just an unfortunate sporting incident in a keenly fought competition. Granted, in the heat of the moment Jarvis may have been 'hot-headed', unfortunately the same can't be said of Daley any more."

Smedley, who went on to win the competition once the track had been cleaned of blood, received a caution and was fined two weeks pocket money.

pinxit

ATHLETE'S HAMMER THROW KILLS THREE

Dorking International Athletics Stadium:

Promising young decathelete Javis Smedley found himself at the centre of a third tragic incident in as many weeks when three participants in the international athletics event were sliced in two by a wayward hammer throw last night.

A traumatised judge at the event described the scene. "All of a sudden, I heard an eerie screech – like a banshee – from the competitors' warm-up area. Before I could turn round, a hammer whizzed past my ears and scythed through the three poor lads, wrapping itself round all three of them like an Argentinian bolo. They didn't stand a chance. The wire sliced them in two at the waists like a cheese-cutter."

One stunned spectator said: "Jarvis was like that Tasmanian Devil from the cartoons! He seemed hysterical, laughing as he stooped over their carved up bodies – and – I think he spat on them!"

Sombre GB coach and Smedley's mentor, Stuart Broad said: "It was a schoolboy error. Jarvis is only 16 and simply hadn't put enough talcum powder on his hands to get proper purchase on the hammer. It's nearly 8 kilos of solid lead y'know, not easy to control with the long wire and heavy grip. He was going through his swinging routine and accidentally released it. He's very upset and he immediately went over to say sorry to the lads. He was so upset he was crying as he bent over them."

"Ok, I'll admit he is a wee bit rash at times, but would you want to take that competitiveness out of a Tyson or a Rooney? Of course not! They're all greats, masters of their sports and total nut... er, winners. At this elite level of sport there's a fine line between the fiercely competitive and the maniacally homicidal. Jarvis just has to learn where that line is."

"Ever since he was a nipper, he's been brought up on the Shankly maxim that 'sport isn't a matter of life and death – it's much more important than that'. Only, with Jarvis, it just seems to be 'death' at the moment." said Broad.

At the time of the incident the hapless competitors, two Russians and a Lithuanian, were occupying the first three places in the competition, with Smedley lying fourth.

Bearing in mind the other previous incidents of the last few weeks when two of Smedley's fellow decathletes had been impaled with a javelin and decapitated by a discus, the GB Athletics ruling body imposed a fine of one month's pocket-money, a caution to be 'more careful next time' and ordered Smedley to attend an approved IOC anger-management course for a morning.

Broad went on to say: "To heap a hefty fine or ban the boy is ridiculous. It's not as if he's taken drugs or anything to bring this great sport into disrepute. Jarvis is a serious medal prospect at the next Olympics. The fact that he won today's contest is testament to that."

pinxit

'DEADLY' SMEDLEY TO GO TO OLYMPICS AFTER 'SPEAR' SCARE

Despite a traumatic build-up which has left five fellow athletes dead, promising young decathlete Jarvis Smedley will be representing Great Britain at the Olympic Games, the team GB Athletics selectors announced today.

16 year old Dorking-born Smedley has been at the centre of several athletics track tragedies in the build up to the games within the last month, involving a discus decapitation, javelin impaling and a fatal hammer throw – resulting in the deaths of five of his fellow competitors.

"The setbacks of the last month haven't dented Jarvis' confidence or focus at all," Smedley's coach Stuart Broad said.

"Despite the bad luck to his fellow athletes, he's won all his events. The lad's okay with all the press flak and even quite likes the 'Deadly' Smedley tag they've given him. He's undergone a mornings anger-management course and promised to be 'more careful' in future. So we've drawn a line in the sand pit."

Only last week another tragedy was averted when a judge noticed in the warm up for the pole-vault section of the decathlon event that Smedley's pole was sharpened to a fine point at one end.

"It could have been fatal" said the official. "Imagine Jarvis sprinting down the run-up at 20mph with a 17-foot perpendicular sharpened pole just inches from the other competitors – they would have been kebabbed?"

Coach Broad explained that Smedley had whittled the pole to gain more purchase and thrust into the box in the 'plant' phase of the vault and was unaware it was against the regulations.

Looking forward to the games and the decathlon event, Broad summed up the prospects for his charge. "He's got a chance, but realistically, the three guys ahead of him on the rankings from Austria, Germany and the USA look pretty much nailed on for the medal spots."

"But mark my words, all his competitors are well aware of Jarvis and what he's done...er, achieved in the last few weeks. I'd go so far as to say that the leading guys are all looking over their shoulders in fear."

pinxit

NEWS FROM SUNNYDAZE RETIREMENT HOME.

Oh look a budgie! Isn't it lovely, I had one just like it, a ginger tom it was, but it got run over. Well they did in those days didn't they – not like now, what with all of the clothes that everybody wears, and the different haircuts.

I don't know what the world is coming to, what with all this sex and violence you see nowadays. My Charlie was never like that. Proper gentleman he was – except when he used to tie me to the mangle and hit me with the coal shovel. I blame those mobile phones myself, they've made life too easy for the youngsters, what with colour displays and personalised ringtones and all. We had to know when to press button A or button B when we used the telephone, otherwise the door of the phone box wouldn't open, and you'd be stuck in there with only powdered egg to eat until a policeman came along.

Talking of policemen; Doctor Mangawanga says that he has never seen a cyst like the one on my neck that shape before. He says that I'm a medical abnormality. *"You're a medical abnormality,"* he says to me, and what with my bad leg, I doubt that I'll be able to get down to the chemist's on Wednesday. A martyr to that leg I am. Doreen Ekerslike always said that hers were on upside-down, but I think that was because she was looking at them from above. She was ever so much fun when she got going, except when she drank too much and tried to steal your husband. But I shouldn't speak unkindly of her, now that she's passed over to the other side .... near the greengrocer's just behind the bus station.

They've put new bins in there. Horrible great big ugly things they are, and the people they used to install them! Well, talk about the League of Nations, it was like listening to one of those pop songs where they just shout at you. I'm sure some of them were Welsh.

Do you remember when the bombers used to come over? Terrible it was, sitting in an Anderson Shelter every night waiting for it to start, and not being able to do anything but just grit your teeth and take it. My Charlie used to come back from the pub and pretend to be a German parachutist. Didn't half put the willies up me, I can tell you. He used to make me put on his Home Guard battledress, and would say *"For you Tommy, ze war is over,"* when he was doing the necessary from behind. I don't know what happened to him. He went out for a loaf of bread in 1962, and I haven't seen him since, but at least my piles got better. Not like my bladder, that's never been right since they devalued the pound.

And another thing; They've started giving us those cheap biscuits that you get from the supermarket with the funny name. They go all soggy when......you..............zzzzzzz.................zzzzzzzz.

GM

TROUBLE FLARES AS TUBBIES SLUG IT OUT OVER LAST CHEESEBURGER

Local kebab, pizza and burger entrepreneurial tycoon, Ali Bullo, today revealed how an unsavoury incident involving one of his burger vans in the early hours of this morning, ruined what had hitherto been an excellent evening's trading.

The van concerned, run by one of Ali Bullo's employees, cousin Mikhmash, located in a lay-by on the A27 had enjoyed lively trade throughout the evening, selling almost all of its stock by 2.30 am.

Cousin Mikhmash had only a single cheeseburger left to sell, when he decided to pack up for the night and go to his bed, a soiled mattress by a sink in a room above a kebab shop in Fratton.

It was just as cousin Mikhmash was closing the serving hatch, when four vehicles pulled into the lay-by, disgorging their occupants, who all made a bee line for the burger van.

Mikhmash takes up the story:

"There was about twelve of them all together, in two different groups. Them looking like they been clubbing and had got munchies. Them all very big people innit. Very chunky. Big tubby-chubby types, boys and girls. Them talk loud too. Them come to serving hatch and ask for cheeseburgers – I tell them I have only one cheeseburger, and them all wanting it."

Mikhmash went on to relate how the two groups then got embroiled in a massive argument over who had arrived first, and who was the first in line with a legitimate right to purchase the single remaining cheeseburger.

"Them start shouting," Mikhmash told us. "The lye-dees was the worst. First is shouting, then is them starting pushing. Two of them worst. Two big chunky lye-dees in short dresses them start to chest bump – bouncing off each others boobies and calling terrible swearing names over who have last cheeseburger. Is very traumatic for me. It remind me of Hayling Island gun battle over last mixed kebab. Me cook last cheeseburger because me scared. Them pushing and argument in front of serving hatch and make van unstable. Me keep head down and flip burger..."

It seems that when Mikhmash finally served the last cheeseburger, a full scale brawl erupted as one of the chubby blokes grabbed the last cheeseburger and tossed a five pound note on the counter.

Although there were no serious injuries reported, passing motorists called 999 to report a brawling pile of semi-naked fat people who were effectively tearing the clothes off one another's backs in combat over the last cheeseburger. Police reported large semi-naked ladies with exposed G-strings and acres of bouncing, wobbling cholesterol reinforced flesh, and fat blokes with hugely bloated beer bellies trying to hold their trousers up with one hand whilst aiming punches with the other.

The conflagration apparently ended when the last cheeseburger got knocked from somebody's grasp and fell to the ground, where somebody trod on it, rendering it inedible.

"It was all just bladdy silly really innit"? Mikhmash opined.

We leave the last word with Ali Bullo:

"It can be dangerous, running burger van. Sometimes staff fear for them life innit. This why they am true heroes. And why I pay them three pound an hour, no questions asked."

Skoob 1999

MAN SPOTS TRAIN

In a week when it was feared that *The Dorking Review* would have to close its doors for the last time due to a paucity of things to report, the situation was dramatically saved when local man, Kevin Smally casually mentioned in passing that he had spotted the 12.32 from Rochester yesterday, and that it was **3 minutes late!**

"I had been looking out of my window at the railway line when I saw the train pass," said the dynamic senior citizen. "I always make a cup of tea at the same time each day, and the train invariably passes when the cup is half empty, but this time I had not only drunk all of my tea, but was on my second chocolate biscuit. I checked the clock and it was definitely 3 minutes late. I then verified that the clock was accurate by...........blah, blah, blah........I normally wave to the driver, but they very rarely wave back, but 40 years in the civil service has taught me that not only.........Blah, blah, blah, blah............The locomotive unit was a Cammel 2473 type C, and I noticed that the window frames that were fitted to the front of the driver's cabin were not of the current specification, as laid down by................Drone, drone, blahdee, blahdee, blah................The wife used to joke that I would be buried under a train. Before she left me that is. Anyway, many people think that the type D was far superior to the type C, but they forget that the construction methods used at Crewe varied in a number of significant areas, not least in......................Blahdee, blahdee, blah blah.............................and that's how I got the evidence that Camilla takes it up the arse.

GM

NEW KENTUCKY FRIED PANDA RESTAURANT OPENS DESPITE PROTESTS.

The controversial new fast food eatery, Kentucky Fried Panda, had its grand opening this afternoon despite protests from PETA and other environmental groups.

Although this new fast food restaurant looks like any other of its kind, it's the menu in this eatery that's causing the uproar. Every menu item at Kentucky Fried Panda features one of the world's most endangered species ... pandas.

The purveyor of Kentucky Fried Panda, Confucius Wong-Dong was anxious to describe the menu to us in more detail. In fact, we couldn't stop him. No matter how hard we tried.

"Our panda seasoned with mix of 23 herbs and spices. We fry panda, douse panda in soy sauce and then serve panda to customer. Tasty! We have panda-burger where we put regular fried panda on bread with ketchup. Tasty! We have sweet-sour fried panda soup; panda rolls, fried panda wedges and lots more. Tasty!"

When asked if he had anything 'panda-free' on the menu, Mr Wong-Dong shook his head vehemently. "No. Everything have panda. Even soda have panda. Tasty!"

Understandably, PETA is very unhappy about the opening of

Kentucky Fried Panda. "This is a nightmare. I can't believe this is even happening," said PETA member Forrest Brooks.

"I mean, there are only, like, 13 pandas left on Earth. Where the hell is he getting them from"?

PETA and other unwashed hippie types are planning protests like sit-ins, picketing and possible fire-bombing until KFP is shut down and Mr Wong-Dong is arrested.

A Panda Plate (a helping of fried panda, sweet and sour panda soup and a panda roll – drink not included) costs 149.99. Tasty!

Madame Bitters

CAR BOOT SALE A BIT OF A LET DOWN

The inaugural car boot sale held in the grounds of St Juste The Same school in Frigghall On Sea turned out not to be quite the money spinning cash cow the organisers had hoped for.

Mayor Sully Birdkrapp expressed his disappointment that only nineteen cars, a burger van and a bouncy castle had shown up, blaming local by-laws which stipulate that any such event must be staged between four and nine a.m.

"It was just too early," Mayor Birdkrapp explained. "But we couldn't really do anything about it because of the by-laws. Most people were still in bed by the time the vendors were packing up, and those that did come were disappointed. Even though we had northern comedy duo Cannon and Ball to cut the ribbon. We haven't given up on the idea yet, but we appreciate that changes need to be made."

Potential customer, Jason Wrist, from nearby Twattington On The Bog, who drove the five miles to the car boot sale with his civil partner Graham, was very disappointed by what he found. He told us:

"It was rubbish. Graham and I got up at two thirty so we'd be the first here. We were hoping to pick up some rare objets d'art, perhaps a nice throw rug, or a pair of matching silk kimonos, but there was nothing like that on sale. It was just broken tape recorders, old VHS tapes, boxes of coat- hangers, cracked plates, and old hammers and saws. And some knock-off DVD's. It was only the burger van that made the trip worthwhile. It was nice meeting Cannon and Ball, but to be honest, they're a bit passé."

Burger van proprietor and kebab shop entrepreneur Ali Bullo told us:

"It was big wash out. Me no come again. Me sell only six burgers, two of them, egg burgers, to some gay bloke looking for silk kimono. What that all about? Me no come back. Selling six burgers is no bladdy good. No even pay for petrol. Car boot sale my arse."

Stall-holder Mike Melody, was a little more upbeat, telling our reporter that he'd certainly come back again, adding:

"Not a bad days graft that. I shifted a Chucky doll off the Child's Play video nasties for forty four quid. I was made up getting rid of that. It gave me the creeps anyway."

Mayor Birdkrapp is keeping his fingers crossed that Frigghall On sea's next planned civic extravaganza, a mass guided tour of the mud flats, will prove more popular. More as we get it.

Skoob 1999

MISSING SPADE FOUND IN GARDEN SHED

The home of avid garden tool collector Wilfred Trimble of Pyle Street Dorking was broken into last Saturday. Nothing was taken except a rare and valuable antique 1897 Spear and Jackson 'Turf Scorcher' spade from his collection.

"It was the prize item in my collection," said Mr Trimble, who readers will remember found it by chance on sale at a local auction house two years ago

A trembling Mr Trimble told us: "To most people it was just a spade, but to those in the know, such a spade with a 3' 6" X 2" ash handle and the overturned sole protectors on a hand-forged case- hardened steel blade, together with the brass inlayed maker's mark and brass number three screws in the handle could only mean one thing........

The S&J Turf Scorcher, 'Holy Grail of Spades' – all collectors dream of having one."

Mr Trimble was able to buy it at the knock-down price of £2.50 at Bidder's Auction House in Carisbrooke Road because only he knew what it really was.

He then took his prize spade, worth perhaps as much as £35 to spade connoisseurs, and put it with the 225 others in his extensive collection, to be regularly admired.

He told us at the time: "I'll never sell it, not for all the tea in China. In tool collecting circles we call it the 'Ace of Spades'.

There it stayed until last Saturday's break-in.

A bereft Mr Trimble had put announcements in the press and on local radio pleading for the rare item to be returned because it was of such sentimental value. He even offered a reward of £4.75 for information leading to its safe return.

Jail Break

Police had been investigating the disappearance of the spade all week, however, resources had been limited by the escape from prison of Rastus Winston O'Leary who escaped two weeks ago and which lead to a nation-wide dragnet operation, high alert at all ports and reinforcements of three more constables being drafted in from Guildford.

The public had been warned that O'Leary, serving thirty years for crimes involving poultry, was dangerous, should not be approached under any circumstances and to call the police immediately if seen.

Only one constable was available to investigate the Trimble break-in, yet by the strangest of coincidences, Constable Wayne Scales was able both to apprehend the fugitive and to recover the stolen property.

"I received a phone call from a Dorking resident Mr Albert Hall reporting that he had a spade, so I went to investigate, although I didn't think that it would amount to much from the information I had been given," said Constable Scales to our reporter.

Hidden in shed

Here, in the words of 75 year old Mr Albert Hall of 27 Carisbrook Road are the dramatic circumstances surrounding the arrest of the fugitive and the recovery of the spade:

"Well it was the missus see, my Winnie, she sees in the paper about this spade some bloke wants, £4.50 'e wanted ter pay fer it! 'Ere Winnie, I sez, we got a spade 'ent we? Well I can't say I uses it since me back went an all that, so I thought I'd ring the number ter see if the spade could do someone a faver see? An' £4.50 can buy a nice fish supper. Anyhow the copper comes knockin' an' I sez to 'im I sez, go 'ave a look in the shed cos that's where the spades is. Next thing I knows there's this almighty ruckus and Constable Scales comes aht o' the shed with a spade in one 'and and a black geezer kickin' up a fuss in the other. Lucky the copper was a big bloke an' could 'andle spades. Although I thought it a bit funny cos the spade dint even look like my one. Then 'e told me wot it was all abaht so I does as 'e asks and phones the station fer a van ter cart the villain orf in. When 'e told me who it was 'e'd collared that explained everyfink. - I fort next door's chickens 'ad bin makin' funny noises in the night, well they would wunt they, specially if O'Leary was finkin' of diggin' under the wire."

O'Leary up before the Beak

The court heard from psychiatrist Dr Henman on the subject of Ornithological Onanism, the condition suffered by O'Leary. In O'Leary's case it was so severe that he had requested that court officials and policemen refrain from any mention of 'Beaks' and that foam instead of feather mattresses be provided in the cells during detention to avoid problems.

He also described O'Leary's lapse into a life of crime as tempted by others who told him that it didn't matter if he got caught because he could 'do as much bird as he liked inside'. However, his condition had not deteriorated to the extent that it might have done and there was still hope that with psychotherapy and medication he could be kept stable.

The Court was reminded of the severity of such psychoses by mention of the historic examples from 1928 of the Dudley dog rogerer, the 1943 Badger bugger of Bridport (bearing in mind it was wartime) and, nearer home, the more recent mysterious goings-on with cattle in Reigate that nobody but the perpetrator ever seemed to have got to the bottom of.

Summing-up, Dorking Magistrate Mr I Sendom-Downe J.P. said:

"Rastus Winston O'Leary, we have heard how you broke into Mr Trimble's house and stole the valuable spade with the intention of running rampage among the local poultry population and intending to hijack a lorry before making your getaway along the A24, no doubt having in mind to wreak more ornithophile havoc and mayhem among avians in neighbouring counties.

"We have heard how you lay in wait in the shed with this perverted intention, and how only Mr Hall's desire to help out a fellow human in his hour of need led to your arrest by a brave and doughty officer of the law. It was only that selfless act on the part of Mr Hall that led to such a valuable spade not sustaining irreparable damage.

"Had you not been apprehended, who knows what other horrors you might have perpetrated? The public and its livestock are not safe as long as you are at large. It pains me to say that sentencing is not the responsibility of the Court since you will be delivered into the custody of the Prison Authorities who will then deal with the escape according to proper procedure and sentence for the current crimes will be passed at the Winchester Quarter Sessions.

"I can only hope that it means a long extension to your current term of incarceration, and also that as you purge your sentence you will be kept a very long way from the Prison Farm and the Governor's Budgerigar. Do you have anything to say for yourself before you are taken down?"

In a last ditch attempt at mitigation O'Leary's solicitor, Mr I Grabbit LLB, said that his client was deeply repentant for having stolen the spade and wanted to own up also to having broken into two other chicken runs in Newport and a cattery in Carisbrook and asked that four other fences be taken into consideration.

Sighs of relief. Safe returns and just rewards.

Representatives of *The Dorking Review* were allowed to return the spade to an excited Mr Trimble who presented Mr Hall with his just reward of £4.75. As Mr Trimble replaced his beloved S&J Turf Scorcher next to the other 225 garden spades in his collection, they mused that O'Leary was once again safely locked in his cell and only able to watch from behind bars, the seagulls, sparrows and pigeons wheeling safe from harm in the sky. Albeit, like Mr Trimble, with a mysterious dark, moist patch spreading like an ink blot on the front of his trousers.

(The RSPB have announced that they have now stood-down the armed guard on the duck colony at the local pond and that it is once again open to visitors.)

LC

MISSING DORKING 'TRICK OR TREATERS' MYSTERY DEEPENS

Police say that they are still investigating every avenue in their search for the three missing 'Trick or Treat' teenagers who terrorized elderly and disabled pensioners in a care home condominium on the quiet leafy streets of Dorking two nights ago.

"It's a mystery alright." said Police Chief Carpenter as his team finished questioning the last of the frightened senior citizens subjected to the gang's attacks and threats. "These boys just seem to have disappeared off the face of the earth."

"They weren't just 'pesky kids' asking for candy, those hoodlums were operating an organised protection racket," said frail 93 year-old wheelchair-bound widow Mrs Norma Bates. "They wanted the keys to cars, our TVs, cell phones and jewellery. Firecrackers through the door, bricks through the windows, threatening, sneering and cussing us. We were all terrified. Poor Mr Lecter filled his colostomy bag in less than five seconds."

Mrs Bates went on to say that despite 999 calls to the local police, no help arrived. "In the end, it got so bad Frederick went to the door to confront them. Good riddance to their sorry lil' hoodie asses is what I say!"

Frederick, a thin, frail and badly scarred gentleman in his 80's was understandably vague on the subsequent events.

"I don't recollect for sure," he grimaced, boney fingers and long, unkempt fingernails coming up to his trilby hat in the modest and courteous manner of a less troubled age. "Let's just say I have a feeling those young gentlemen won't be getting up to any more mischief in Elm Street."

Next of pumpkin have been informed.

pinxit

LOCAL MAN WINS CAR

Lucky local man, Kevin Nobbart was presented with the keys of a shiny new Ford Focus yesterday, which was the star prize in the High Street Motors Grand Raffle.

A delighted Mr Nobhart (who already has a company car of his own) attended the High Street Motors showroom along with his dowdy looking wife Sharon (who has one of those little Audis) and his two children to collect his prize. "I am absolutely over the moon" he said; "I never thought that I would win."

The new car boasts an array of optional extras and should give Mr Nobhard many years of trouble free motoring. It also came complete with a year's road fund licence and a full tank of fuel, although it was impossible to know if it was insured. There certainly wasn't an insurance company sticker in the window and he must have been quick off the mark to arrange it before he arrived at the showroom.

Nobhead, who unlike many other people who had bought up to 14 tickets, and their girlfriends who had bought at least 5, won the car when his one and only ticket was drawn last Thursday. He now has the luxury of a choice of cars to use each morning, unlike some of us who have to take the bus to the *Review* offices each day, and get piss-wet through while waiting for it, because the clutch on our Renault 25 is fucked.

He was handed the keys of his new car by Mr John Hartman, the Managing Director of High Street Motors, whom I'm sure he went to school with. Not the same year, but they may well have met, and it wouldn't surprise me one little bit if they were related by marriage. A celebratory glass of champagne was drunk before the Knobheads and their insufferable children skulked off in their new possession.

It is believed that one of the people attending the ceremony acting out of concern for public safety, tipped off the police that the driver of the car had been drinking, but unfortunately they failed to turn up to arrest the bastard.

All of the reporters and staff at *The Dorking Review* send their congratulations.

GM

CHINESE BLOKE DIES IN 'EEL UP THE BUM' PRANK GONE WRONG

When Chinese chef Lee Kee Woof got a bit bladdered on beer and rice wine the other day, he had no idea that the consequences of his binge would leave him dead; Or he probably wouldn't have done it.

As Lee Kee Wolf passed out from his excess, his mates at the restaurant where he worked thought it would be a really hilarious prank to stick a foot long live eel up his arse.

Amid much Chinese related hilarity, Woof's friends also eventually passed out. When they eventually came round, the drunken young chef was dead.

An ambulance was called, but Woof was pronounced dead on arrival at the local hospital. A post mortem examination revealed that the eel, which was still alive when it was extracted from Woof's arse had eaten half of his bowels, and that the young chef had died from massive internal bleeding.

A spokesman for British charity organisation: Drink But Be Careful, told us:

"Tragic case. Tragic. This just goes to show that sticking things up your mate's arse when he's munted can have fatal consequences. It was really bloody stupid of them to stick a live, foot long eel up this man's arse. It was basically a death sentence. The thought of having a foot long eel stuffed up your arse isn't a nice thought at the best of times. I can only advise drunken fools not to stick things up their mates arses. Eels are lethal, as are power tools, grandfather clocks, statues of horses and car engines."

A sobering thought indeed.

More as we get it.

Skoob 1999

Reviews

REVIEW: KING EDWARD POTATOES

In my capacity as a top reviewer, I was recently sent a bag of fifteen King Edward potatoes to review.

My initial reaction was one of disappointment, as there was no instruction manual in the bag. The web address printed on the side took me to a national supermarket chain, where I still could not find any instructions on how to use these potatoes.

Being a dedicated reviewer, I used a well known search engine and entered the phrase "What are King Edward Potatoes for"? Whereby I located a kind of instruction manual for the product. According to the site I should have also received a 'potato peeler' with the potatoes, as this appears to be a vital tool for using King Edwards. I eventually located a 'potato peeler' in my cutlery drawer of all places! Having already checked the more logical places, such as under the stairs and the garage.

There were no instructions on how to use the 'potato peeler', but before and after pictures were provided on the website, and although I took off as much skin from my fingers as from the potatoes, a quick wash to remove the blood left the King Edward matching the 'after' picture.

With a now denuded potato, I was still at a loss as to what it was for, so I returned to the internet and discovered that it was ideal for 'mashing' apparently. Not having a 'potato masher' even in my cutlery drawer, I used a hammer. This broke the King Edward into smithereens, but the final result did not match the 'light and fluffy' picture on the website.

I tried the peeling process again with another of the potatoes, removing much less skin this time, either because I had less to start with, or because I was getting better at this tricky art that really should be taught in schools. The next option on the site was 'roast potato'. It took several minutes with my blow-lamp to turn the potato into the image on the website. The website itself described the interior as 'light and fluffy', a recurring theme on the site. The potato now appeared to be too hot to hold, revealing to me the source of the phrase "Hot potato." Using my jigsaw, I was disappointed to discover that the interior of my potato was identical to how it had started, more hard and slimy than light and fluffy; additionally it damaged a jigsaw blade when the potato skittered across the workbench.

Resolving to have one last go, I selected a third potato. The website said that the King Edward was perfect for chips – again, there were no instructions on how to go from unpeeled potato to chipped potato. As I was also currently reviewing a tree chipper at the time I used this, and it did a fantastic job, although the resulting pieces were not as evenly sized as in the picture and had not turned a golden yellow colour. Upon using a hacksaw to open one (I had run out of jigsaw blades), the interior was still not 'light and fluffy', but resolutely identical to how it had started.

I can only give King Edward Potatoes one star, due to the lack of instructions and sheer dangerous nature of them. They should only be handled by experts, and are not suitable for the man in the street. The tree chipper review will be submitted once the skin has grown back on my fingers.

IB

THE PRE-RAPHAELITES AND ITALY
EXHIBITION – ASHMOLEAN MUSEUM

The Pre-Raphaelite Brotherhood was highly influenced by Italian art and literature. We sent our art historian **Proserpine Gainsborough-Halfwit** *to run an eye over the current exhibition of Pre-Raphaelite art at Oxford's Ashmolean.*

"Review the Pre-Raphaelite thing at the Ashmolean," the boss said. "It finishes next month."

"Of course – great. I love the Pre-Raphs," I said, "Where's the Ashmolean – can I get a taxi?"

"It's in Oxford – and if you get a taxi from London, you're paying. Train fare only on expenses," he said.

Oxford!

After spending hours on the internet, I learned I could get a train (a train! I mean...) from Ealing Broadway without having to traipse into Paddington on a Saturday. Yuck!

So I spent an hour and forty minutes on a horrid little local-type train which stopped at every horrid little halt in those west-of-London suburbs and some other places I'd never heard of. (Didcot Parkway, anyone?)

(Oh yes – and a humungous 'thank you' to everyone in the office for **NOT** telling me that if I'd changed at Slough I could've got a faster train from there! You really are all *so* mean.)

So I got a taxi from the station (ugh – hundreds of ordinary people!) and the editor is refusing to pay for that: "It's not five minutes bloody walk," he says.

"But I was a girl alone in a strange city!"

"It was bloody Oxford on a bloody Saturday in broad daylight you stupid bloody…"

So, 'The Pre-Raphaelites and Italy.' Full of stupid people, of course. I don't know why I bother. You can never get near the pictures at these things. People peering short-sightedly at the brushwork, or some minute detail.

And screaming toddlers bored out of their wits.

And pseudy-arty-looking types standing for simply *ages* in front of a picture you want to look at, pretending they're pondering the painterliness of the work when really you know they're thinking about what's for dinner. They know you're waiting, but they refuse to budge.

There were some Rossetti water colours and some of his later portraits, but in between there was some really (really) dull stuff by Ruskin – his paintings of bits of Italian architecture. Plus, he doesn't really count as a Pre-Raphaelite, does he?

Some of Burne-Jones' designs for some church or other also helped to fill one of the three rooms.

But it's not a very large show and I certainly wondered why they bothered putting it together... Rossetti was the most featured painter here and he never even went to Italy, despite his family background and fascination with Dante!

Anyway, a nice man at the station told me about changing trains on my way back to Ealing Broadway, so my journey home was just an hour (so yah booh to everyone in the office).

I think I will go back to the Ashmolean one day. But someone will have to drive... I'll get Jeremy to take me! Or Ben in his Beamer!

SM

WOMEN ARE FROM URANUS

The publishing world and authors of self-help books alike have been turned on their respective ears by the new number one best-selling non-fiction book: Women Are From Uranus.

The unlikely author of this self-help book is Leland "Blackie" Blackheart, a former rock quarry worker who is currently on disability.

When Blackheart, who has an 8th grade education, was asked what made him qualified to give romantic advice he gave a startling answer. "Well" said Blackheart as he leaned back in his lawn chair and worked a pinch of chewing tobacco between his cheek and gum. "It's like this y'see, I've always had a knack at getting the ladies. I been married four times and have had a bunch of girlfriends, usually when I was married at the time. You tell me that don't take some talent. Hell, I got everyone from twelve year old boys to seventy year old men, and everyone in between askin' me how I do it; what my secret is. So I figgured, why not write all this down, so I don't gotta keep repeatin' myself. Now, readin' and writin' was never my thing, so I got one of my girlfriends to write it up for me. Missy's real smart; she went to beauty school and nearly graduated. Then we went to the library, made a bunch of copies and sold them for $15.00 each."

One of the buyers, Wade Munson, was so happy with the results following the advice that Blackheart gave him that he told his brother-in-law who owns a small printing company – Outhouse Press, all about it. Blackheart's book was printed up, and before long, major publishing house, Simon and Schuster took notice and jumped at the opportunity to buy Blackheart's book. Peter Smalls, the president of Simon and Schuster was noted as saying: "Well, when we got hold of the book we were very excited. We knew we had something...unique. The spelling, grammar and everything else was pretty rough, but we knew we had something ground-breaking."

Molly Clovis who edited Blackie's book added: "Blackheart's original book was really more of a list. When we first got it, it was only five pages long and needed more content. So we put some of our best ghostwriters on the job and they filled out Blackheart's book to 450 pages. The finished product was; Women Are From Uranus."

Some of Blackheart's advice within the book includes:

*When you and your woman are at Dairy Queen, make sure you order for her. Women don't know what they want, ever. They'll thank you, probably with a blow job.

*Treat your woman like a queen at first but not for too long. You don't want to spoil her.

*Woman like a man who can be a gentleman. Offer to pay for her burger. Open doors for her. Offer to undo your own cutoffs.

*When your woman has her "lady days" and she starts crying about something, tell her: "You look fat when you cry," so she'll stop. If she won't stop, go out for a beer with your buddies to give her some alone time.

*Women, if you want to get a man, tell him you think he's the most handsome, studly and smartest man in the world as soon as you meet him. Then take him back to your trailer, put your kids outside and then lay it on him.

This unorthodox self-help book on relationships has taken the book-buying public by storm, but it has many critics, most of whom are experts on relationships. Dr Winstone Claptrap is one expert of many who decry Blackheart's book. He has this to say about it: "Mr Blackheart is an unemployed former quarry worker with an eighth grade education. He's been divorced four times, with his last failed marriage ending in his attempted murder. He is suspected of fathering as many as eleven children but refuses to acknowledge or care for any of them." He go's on to say, "Leland Blackheart is the *last* person to give advice on relationships – or anything else for that matter."

Mr Blackheart himself doesn't take any of this criticism seriously. "Look, I know what works and I'm rakin' in the money hand over fist," he says. "And besides, I had two girls last night. At the same time *and* without havin' to pay for 'em. Why don't you ask them doctors when the last time they got some was"?

The doctors refused to comment.

Madame Bitters

SHE-WOLVES: THE WOMEN WHO RULED ENGLAND BEFORE ELIZABETH, BY HELEN CASTOR

Before Elizabeth I became the iconic 'Virgin Queen', four women ruled England in what was very much a man's world. Medievalist Dr Castor examines their stories.

Ken Lucid *writes*:

So. OK? I'm reviewing a book about women. Satisfied?

I'm not kidding you, round here it's "women this, women that." It's not enough that we include the feminine side in our various modules and courses, we have set aside whole modules to the feminine.

So, like, we can't just do "Bismark, Little Germans and the Unification of Germany." Oh no! We have to have something called "Bismark's Distaff: Women and the Unification."

I don't know – *you* try to put together an hour's lecture on Clara Schumann and the struggle against Austria-Hungary!

And it's not even enough that you tell a bunch of uninterested undergrads about the downfall of Napoleon III and the Second Empire thanks to Bismark's plans. The sisterhood wants to know what happened to Empress Eugenie! Why? "She went to live at Farnborough and then Chislehurst...OK?"

Strewth!

Anyway, this young historian is a fellow at Sidney Sussex, Cambridge, and she knows how to tell a story. It's not my period, but she seems to know what she's talking about.

Might look her up next time we're at the same conference.

Oh yeah – the women in the book are Matilda, Eleanor of Aquitaine, Isabella (Edward II's wife) and Margaret of Anjou. What happened to Bloody Mary?

Ken Lucid is professor of Modern History at the University of Thames Valley East.

SM

HAIRLESS 200XL HI-FI CABLE

I must admit I was sceptical when I first received this cable for review from Hairless Hi-Fi Cable Company. At £500 a metre it seemed a little expensive.

This unidirectional, quasi-fluxed gold connection cable has the usual quantum tunnelling, light wave amplification and electrical dampening properties hi-fi buffs have come to know and love in the higher-end bracket, but in addition, it is dishwasher safe and can be used as an emergency tow-rope. Surprisingly, it can also be used as a toe-rope for the lexicographically challenged. With its Vibration Dampening technology, it not only improves a standard hi-fi, but will also improve video reception in a television *without even being plugged in to the TV.* According to the literature, you do not even need to own a TV for it to be improved; a claim I could not verify as I own a television.

Upon opening the package from the company, my alopecia was instantly cured and my wife became pregnant, despite my vasectomy and her visiting Taiwan at the time. Incredible! It stopped a dimensional rift from forming in my living room, eradicated all the viruses off my computer and unscrambled the encrypted channels on my Freeview decoder. And that was before I connected it to my hi-fi.

Once I had connected it between my hi-fi and amp and switched it on, I, a sceptical phonophobe, was instantly converted. I put in a Michael Hutchins CD and it brought forth his ghost to perform in my living room. The track *Suicide Blonde* prevented the suicide of the blonde who lives in the flat downstairs from me, as she too could feel the pitch-perfect notes as they energised her body. Even when the song had finished, the angelic chorus that soaked from the walls of my flat continued to uplift my soul. When I put on *The White Album* by The Beatles, I received news that John Lennon and George Harrison had faked their deaths, and would be reforming the iconic band and naming their next album after me.

Comparing this cable with the Real-Tones 1200dpi (review elsewhere), although it is half the price, it is easily four times the quality. This cable survived five minutes in my blender, which is more than can be said for the 1200dpi! I also do not recall the 1200dpi preventing a war in East Africa, which was something the Hairless had managed without breaking into a sweat.

I must admit that there was a moment's panic with this product when I connected it back to front, as my speakers started to produce dark matter, and an unholy demonic stench emanated from under my floorboards. However, this was corrected instantly the moment I connected the cable correctly.

In summary, this is THE best cable for sound quality, dimensional rift restructuring and emergency motor-vehicle repair available on the market today. However, I am reluctant to recommend it as they only do it in black. I would have preferred to have had a choice of colours, but this option is unavailable. For this reason, I can only give it four out of five stars.

IB

THE KETCHUP COOKBOOK
BY
SIZEWELL B POWER

Tomato ketchup is one of the most reviled food dressings in the world, especially by chefs, who view the condiment as fit for use only in practical jokes as a source of fake blood.

Yet *The Ketchup Cookbook* by Birmingham-born food writer, Sizewell B Power, has been flying off the shelves as fast as the printers can turn them out.

"They said it couldn't be done," said Power. "They called me a food philistine, but I proved them all wrong. You see, ketchup is everybody's guilty secret. I bet you there's a bottle of ketchup in all the top chef's larders, but of course, they'll deny it. They're all bleedin' liars and hypocrites, that lot."

Power does seem to have a point – hot dogs would be pretty rubbish without ketchup, and the red stuff certainly enhances a ship butty, (sandwich – Ed) and this book lists a myriad of culinary ketchup applications.

Apparently, carrot and coriander soup tastes wonderful with ketchup, as the book points out in its dedicated sections.

Some of the stuff in the book will undoubtedly make the purists go stiff with outrage, such as ketchup on a traditional Sunday roast, fillet steak with ketchup, sea bass with ketchup, vanilla ice cream with ketchup, and apple pie with ketchup.

The book's soaraway success looks all set to turn the epicurean world on its arse.

Skoob 1999

BOOK OF THE DEAD – BRITISH MUSEUM. DISAPPOINTING PLAYING CARDS

We are fascinated by the ancient Egyptians and their death cults. Why? Perhaps this exhibition at the British Museum could explain.

*Archaeologist **Chasuble Mendip-Never** writes:*

To Bloomsbury, the British Museum. Why, oh why? I detest and loathe these things. Rubbing along with the great unwashed, the *hoi polloi,* the mob... Oh, the mob! Bonaparte had the right idea...

And why do so many of them bring their small children? Sigh.

The writing is on the wall, as it were, from the moment we enter the introductory display – entry is by timed tickets, and everyone due to enter at 1.20 has turned up at 1.20 along with late 1.10s. The place is heaving.

I can smell the press of humanity and I find it noisome.

One cannot get close to any part of the display to examine it properly. So tiresome.

Dopey old women and cocky young men stand in front of you while you're reading a caption or examining an exhibit.

I develop a policy of reading each room's introductory 'writing on the wall' and flash-visiting displays that are not too crowded.

In a particularly gruesome space, I stop and look at my fellow viewers. I have just read that souls with whom the gods were displeased would be upended, and thus forced to eat excrement and drink urine ... a thoroughly uncomfortable experience. As was this visit.

And the gift shop playing cards. How dare they?

I have been collecting playing cards for many years and rarely have I been so disappointed by such a souvenir pack.

The court cards repeat the same picture in each suit and the aces are, likewise, all the same. Even the standard pack we all use for patience and bridge manages to display different king, queens and knaves in each suit.

Lacking foresight and thus oblivious that we would be rubbing salt in my wounds, my wife and I decided to take a late lunch in the Museum Tavern across the road.

Marvellous Timothy Taylor Landlord bitter, really well kept. But a "sharer" plate of nachos is quite enragingly *sans* jalapenos – although the French lady at the adjacent table had so many she left more than she could have consumed.

No, reader, I was not tempted.

I can't blame the museum for jalapeno deficiency. But I have a mind too.

SM

PARTY FOOD

Having sent off my latest review, I sat wondering what I could review next when a blue delivery van pulled up outside with a delivery for me. I accepted the four boxes from the lady driver called Tess Coe or something similar, and took them inside to see what I would be reviewing.

Judging by the contents, I would be reviewing party food. First out of the box were small sausages. They were very nice and easily should be included in any party where vegetarians are otherwise catered for; although as they were pork sausages, I felt that their inclusion was discriminatory towards faiths that prohibit pork.

There were several bags of crisps in a variety of shapes and flavours. Not particularly healthy, but I opened them and sampled a considerable amount of each. My favourites were the Springles. (Cheese and onion flavour – outstanding!) My least favourite were the Hola hoops; they were too firm and I could see many a small child losing a tooth they were saving for the tooth fairy on them. Wotsits were *very* tasty. I finished the oversize bag before I realised that they were gone.

The second box contained party plates, hats, tooter and a table cloth. The plates would have been useful for holding the sausages and crisps had I seen them. I did not like the "Ben 10" design, on them which looked crudely drawn. The table cloth was paper, so I subjected it to some stress tests; wetting a section to simulate spilled juice and then pulling at it. It shredded very easily, so I marked it down. The party hats were all too small for my head, and the elastic snapped far too easily. The tooters were fun for a few seconds, but very quickly lost their squeak.

Box four contained more food. Sausage rolls, ham, bread rolls, carrot sticks, dip and chicken bites. I used the plates and put out the food. There was quite a lot; enough for at least twelve children. I marked them up for quantity. Although I felt quite full by now I continued to sample the foodstuffs, particularly enjoying the chicken bites. If I'd not been stuffed already, I'd probably have finished them.

Overall, I decided that Coe's party food selection was well worth three stars. I'd have given it more, but without anything provided to drink, the food made me rather thirsty. They could also have provided candles, a better table cloth and a cake slice.

I'd also have marked them higher if I'd supposed to have been reviewing them. As it turned out, my son's birthday party was ruined. Look out for my next review when I'll be reviewing divorce lawyers.

IB

IPOD ATTO

Once in a while, as Dorking's top reviewer, I get handed something to review that makes the whole job worthwhile.

This month, I was asked to review the hottest technological product *ever*: the iPod Atto.

The iPod Nano is the slimmed down version of the iPod, which is a slimmed down version of the iPhone or iPad. Or conversely, the iPhone is a beefed up version of the iPod, which is a beefed up version of the iPod Nano. The iPod Atto is everything all of these marvellous inventions are, plus it is tiny.

When I say tiny, I mean minuscule.

I was quite excited when I received the pure brilliant white box with the Apple hologram on the lid. The box itself was about the size of a good thick book, the kind of book that you take on holiday but you know that you won't finish in a week: a Dan Brown or one of the later Harry Potters, although you wouldn't finish them for a completely different reason – because they're rubbish!

With a flick of a tab, the box unfolded using clever origami, which is a nice technological trick in itself, and only served to whet my appetite further. There was the usual Apple box contents: A manual explaining how to open the box, a CD that would only run on an

Apple Mac, a CD that would run on a PC but would tie my PC to Apple for all eternity, a sachet of anti-humidity crystals with "Do not eat you will DIE a horrible death if you do" written in red on it, a list of things I should not do with the Atto, including not using it as a flotation device, and a poster that unfolded to the size of a dining table, with diagrams of the Atto showing its various functions annotated in every language but Mandarin Chinese and English; and finally the Atto itself.

It took several minutes to locate the Atto in the box. Going off one of the pictures on the fold out poster, I knew that it would be rectangular, but there was no sense of scale on the pictures. This lead me to overlook the grain of rice sized technology sitting in a small dimple in the plastic packaging. I had mistaken it for some of the anti-humidity crystals that had leaked out of the sachet.

At the bottom of the box, after everything had been removed was a slab of smoky, vaguely black plastic with a USB cable. This was my Atto's connection to the outside world. I excitedly hooked the slab to my Apple Mac, and loaded the software. As usual the software installed with a single click, choosing to replace most of the software I had downloaded previously with less-able Apple versions I would have to pay for later, and changed the colour of the Mac from white to pink.

I spent twenty minutes looking for the Atto, that I had foolishly put down near the computer, but could no longer find it. It was underneath a chocolate biscuit. After eating the biscuit, taking the crumb off the interface mat and replacing it with the Atto that I thought it was, I had access to the Atto's innards. Swiftly I loaded up a couple of albums without making a dent in its memory. Holding the Atto to my ear, I was surrounded by a beautiful harmonic sound of similar quality to the Hi-Fi in my lounge. Holding it to my eye the Atto projected straight into my retina an uploaded movie in dazzling colours.

I was seriously impressed until I dropped it.

According to the literature, the Atto can be dropped from the top of the Empire State Building and it would still work. How they know this I can't say, because I couldn't find it after dropping it four feet.

I'd love to have given the Atto five stars for the quality and ease of use. However, I've got to pay for it now out of my wages, so it's only going to get one.

I'm never complaining about the iPhone being too big again.

IB

THE END OF BYZANTIUM, BY JONATHAN HARRIS

Constantinople fell to the Turks on May 29, 1453 – the last embers of the Roman Empire were finally extinguished. **Ken Lucid** *considers this latest retelling of the end of a very long story...*

Leeds railway station, Friday morning. A two-and-a-bit hours ride back to London after a conference...Girondins and Jacobins, I seem to remember. Scintillating stuff.

Anyway, I was knackered. Completely worn out – it was a conference with a pretty good night life! I always like a visit to Leeds. I like to try to get one dinner at Whitelock's, an olde worlde pub hidden down an alley off one of the main shopping drags. Wonder if they still do their great pies...

So, I was in my seat on the train anticipating a quiet journey. No work to do, bit of a drink, sleep — you know the score. Anyway, this bloke came and sat opposite me and after settling down he started to talk...and he was a Yank! He could talk Olympics class!

Don't get me wrong, I have a lot of American chums and I love visiting the USA, but this guy was one of those you dread meeting.

He was something to do with household electricals. He blathered on about that for a while and asked me what I did. When I told him I was a historian he went on about the usual rubbish, you know: "I don't know how you remember all those dates...who was it who said 'history is bunk?"

So I forced a laugh and repeated the usual apologetic stuff and reminded him that those who don't learn from history are doomed to repeat its mistakes.

Then I told him I knew something interesting from history that would make him think.

"Do you know how many ways there are to pronounce Byzantine?" I asked him.

"Er, By-zan-tyne...By-zan-teen...Biz-an-teen...Ha. Four or five, I guess," he replies.

"Nope. There are 25."

The next time he opened his mouth, we were pulling in to King's Cross.

"OK," he said, "I got 23."

That was a peaceful ride!

Harris (I don't know him - remarkable, really, since he's a reader at Royal Holloway) has written a very readable account of the siege that led to the fall of Constantinople (this was the Turk's sixth attempt). All of which reminds me...I must go back and read Gibbon again sometime: "Reign and character of Mahomet II ... extinction of the Roman Empire in the East ... " My tatty old copy from student days is propping up a desk somewhere I think. Sacrilege!

Ken Lucid is Chair of History at the University of Thames Valley East.

SM

WHITE LION PUBLIC HOUSE

I found myself with an hour or two to kill in The White Lion off London Road after missing my bus home. The exterior of the property first attracted me to it; it had a roof, and it was raining. There was an advertised beer garden presumably to let me know that all the ales were grown on the premises; additionally, they advertised that they showed every major football match, although I discovered later that this was erroneous.

On entering I approached the bar, which is of the traditional pub style, a little too high to lean on comfortably, and decorated with an array of beer soaked towels. I purveyed the array of beverages on offer from the hand drawn pumps. I asked which of them were grown in the beer garden and received a blank look from the young lady behind the bar, so I selected a pint of *Jeremiad's Regret.* Whilst handing over my money, I enquired about watching the 1973 Unibond minor league cup final that Dorking won 2-1 over Chelmsford. (Possibly my favourite game) only to be told that this wasn't available. So I asked for the Dorking versus Romford game that was happening this weekend instead, only to be told that this wasn't available either. I did point out that they were advertising every major game, and received another blank look, so I took my pint to a seat in the corner.

The room in which I was ensconced was low ceilinged, with dangerous looking beams and a variety of brass items nailed to them, along with a humorous sign about ducking or grousing. There were three other people in the bar area, all men. Previous experience has taught me to avoid looking at other people in pubs; they either hit you, or worse, talk to you. Instead I attempted to do the newspaper crossword, a tricky beast indeed, made more difficult by the table at which I was sat having one leg two inches shorter than the other and being covered in a sticky substance that served no purpose other than ensuring that nobody stole the beer mats.

After finishing the drink, I decided to try another, as there was still some time before my bus arrived. On this occasion, I partook of *Habitual Reminisces*, a flavoursome beer of a deep amber colour. On returning to my table, I discovered that my crossword had been filled in for me and I could no longer lift the newspaper from the table. I read the bar food menu instead, which made me feel a little peckish. I finished my drink quickly and returned to the bar, ordering the lasagne al verde and a pint of *Yelping Buffalo*.

I had somehow managed to make my way through the *Yelping Buffalo* as well as *Hanging Hordes* and *Speckled Tiger* before my lasagne arrived in what can only be described as a thermonuclear container. This was useful as the lasagne was hotter than lava and I could hear the table hissing as I watched the food bubble in unusual colours. My fork started to melt as it approached the food, so I had a *Jalapeno Curse* followed by a *Clicking Cricket*. By point this, my food was cooling enough to ate. Howebber, the flavour it had could be described as tongue destroying, by I atted it, and washed it down with a *Pickled Goat* and an *Unusual Tightrope*. This kept the lasagne from cumming back, but I realised that I'd missed annudder bus, so I had a *Whistling Nun* to pass the time. That was the nicest beer I'd edder ad so I ad two more.

Many more popple ad come in by dis time, and so it took me nearly sevrul minutes to order an *Earphone Calculus*, so wot I fort wus, I'd best order the *Six Six Six* and de *Heated Argument* when I wus dere. The pork scratchings sounded good at dis pint, er point, so I got a bag, and asked if the barmaid had a fone nummer I could ring her on er day off cos she was so attracative. I spose I muss er los it cos I dunno where it is now.

At some point I mussa pissed, er passed out, cos I was back outside getting wet, but me bus come si I got in it and wen ome.

I give The White Lion four out of five stars. It would have got five, but they never did show the football games I'd asked for.

IB

DATING AGENCIES AND RABBIT

As the most dedicated reviewer in Dorking, I occasionally get odd items requiring review. Most recently I was sent the latest in Rabbit's sex toy range: Thrust 2.

However, after the disaster that was the Party Food review that led to my review of divorce lawyers, I have been reviewing local hostelries for the past few months and find myself resolutely single, with no way of testing the Rabbit. There are limits as to how far I'm willing to go in order to review an item, so I had to find a willing partner.

For this reason, I will be combining the review of the sex toy with a review of iHarmony, the on-line dating app from Apple.

Downloading and installing the iHarmony applelet was tricky at first, as I could not locate my iPod Atto, so I borrowed a friend's iPad Nano (or iPhone as it's sometimes called). I installed the applelet on this and completed the easy to use questionnaire. Details such as age, weight, height, eye colour and sexual preference were fairly straightforward, though I did struggle with occupation as General Reviewer was not in the list of available occupations. I settled for General Practitioner as it was the closest alphabetically.

iHarmony has a large database of potential matches, and I was immediately hooked up with five possible dates in my local area, although the applelet's idea of local area did not match mine. I excluded the French girl, despite her attractiveness rating being twelve, and the girl from Leeds. Not due to distance, but because she was a minger. This left me with three potential matches.

While I waited for a response from any of the three, I examined the Rabbit, discovering that it had a pleasant tactile sensation and plenty of options for the lady of pleasure. The model I was testing was a fetching shade of glassy pink. The box stated that it was 'coral'; something I felt was a bad marketing move, as coral is quite sharp and the Rabbit was anything but. It would wiggle, pulse, thrust and vibrate, as well as stimulate the areas a man cannot find without a GPS from Ann Summers. So far so good.

A response through iHarmony came back quickly, which was fortunate as my friend wanted his iPhone back the following morning. I arranged to meet in the town centre at Caffe Nero. It has to be there, as I have been banned from most other places in Dorking. I dressed in a white coat as a doctor would dress, and set off in plenty of time.

The iHarmony service has a unique feature that allows two iPhone owners to find each other, at first using GPS and mapping, and then, when both are in the same crowded room, by shouting "Oi Lover, Over Here!" as you near your potential match. With both of our phones shouting, we approached and touched phones, silencing them.

I was quite impressed with my date for the evening. As her profile suggested, she matched me in terms of interests and also drank coffee, making the location of our first meeting appropriate. We got on very well, even when I revealed that I wasn't a doctor but a reviewer. This was not a problem, as she admitted to a couple of lies on her profile: The first being that she was forty, not twenty two. She asked me what I was reviewing and I decided not to admit to reviewing iHarmony, and instead took out the Rabbit to show her.

This has resulted in my being banned from Caffe Nero as well.

However, my date found this amusing and she excitedly agreed to help me test the Rabbit. Here I discovered her other lie. She was not, as she posted, single. Thus it was back to my bedsit and not her house, as her husband would be home soon.

Together we tried out all of the functions of the Rabbit, discovering the amazing simplicity of the device. It has a very good battery life, and is easy to hold. Being fully adjustable, it provided over an hour of fun for the pair of us, before the review had to end with my date returning home to her husband.

In summary, I can recommend the Rabbit without reservation to any single, married or adulterous women out there. Although I have not used any other sex toys, I cannot see the need for anything other than this device, and I give it an outstanding five out of five stars.

iHarmony is another matter. I am going to give that one star out of five. It works well in respect of ease of set up and matching capabilities but loses marks as there is no way of verifying the information that is provided, and if you forget to un-install it, then the husband of the woman that you met can use her phone to locate you and give you a sound beating. My friend is no longer speaking to me, mainly as he has a broken jaw. However, when his divorce comes through, his wife is very interested in hooking up with me, thanks to the Rabbit.

IB

FEATURES

HOW TO TELL THE DIFFERENCE BETWEEN THE SEXES FOR PHYSICISTS

Many long hours in the lab, observatory, or one's own head can leave many a dedicated physicist unable to make the basic distinction between the sexes.

Fortunately, there is a handy reference for identifying the sexes that can prevent many an unfortunate encounter. This is similar to the process for confirming a hypothesis, and contains many null hypothesis, thus it is totally scientific and can be used without worrying about pesky emotions.

The first step is to check the shoes. Shoes are almost always a great way of identifying men and women from one another. Women have a tendency to wear narrow, shiny and colourful shoes, men wide, matt and dull ones. Mostly, men's shoes are flat, whereas quite often, women's shoes will be heeled, with thin heels.

Shoes are just the first step though. In isolation, they cannot be used to confirm or refute the gender of the person, partly because some men wear high heels, partly because some women wear dull, matt shoes and partly because sometimes staring at people's shoes is rude. A false positive here will generally only result in a woman being classed as a man, which is possibly not a bad thing.

Hair can be a good indication. If the person's hair touches their shoulders, there is a fair chance that they are a woman. Most physicists will only know bald men, but as with swans not all men are bald. Therefore, the hair tenet is a tenuous one; one that MUST be evaluated alongside all other tenets. Quite often, only hair is evaluated, and this has lead to many an awkward moment with somebody who rides a very large motorcycle and has the name Hank.

Habits are a useful method for determining the gender of a person. If they put containers back into the fridge containing just one sip of juice, half a millilitre of milk or a combination of the two in the ketchup bottle, they are a man. If they complain at this being done, they are a woman. This is a certain method for identifying the sexes, but it is hard to garner this information without a restraining order being imposed. Other male habits are wet towels left well away from bathrooms, leaving toilet seats up, and being able to reverse a car. Women's habits include talking, listening and remembering every little thing you ever did wrong.

Clothes, make-up and shape are quite often good identifiers. Trousers can be worn by either sex, but in general, skirts are worn by women. The same is true of make-up (This is facial paint). This is not always the case however. Men who wear skirts and make-up are either transvestites or Scottish. Both will show you a good time, but in very different ways. They can be distinguished by the colour of the make-up – if it is blue they are Scottish. Women tend to have narrower waists than hips, whereas in men it is the other way round. Taking shape, clothes, make-up, hair and shoes together can give a good indication.

The best way of identifying a woman though is yet to be disproved, and has been honoured with the title of "The Law of Sexual Identification." If upon announcing that you are a physicist they say "Wow" they are a man. If they tut and turn away to look for somebody else, they are a woman.

IB

MEN WITH BIG PENISES LIVE LONGER, HAPPIER LIVES

After decades of research by sociologist, psychologists, statisticians, anthropologists and astrologers it has been determined, without any doubt, that men with large penises live longer, happier, more satisfying and productive lives.

"We've suspected it all along, but we needed evidence to support it," said Dr Lester Longdong-Silver of Duke University NC. "Now after all these years we have conclusive proof that well endowed men are happier, live longer and are just generally better than their smaller counterparts."

The study only took into account men who died from natural causes only. Men who died in car accidents, farming and industrial accidents and freak accidents, such as being struck by lightning in a movie theatre were not taken into account. Men who were victims of foul play, be it by a jilted lover who found out her well endowed partner was fooling around with a better looking woman, or by a cuckold husband who catches a well endowed man in mid coitus with his wife, were not counted either.

Strangely enough (or perhaps not) there were no suicides involving men with big penises.

When Dr Longdong-Silver was asked what actually constituted a penis as being large, he simply laughed. "Oh a man knows when he has a large penis. After years of locker rooms and group showers, they know."

When asked if there was any way for smaller men to beat the odds of leading a miserable, pathetic existence, Dr Longdong-Silver shook his head. "No, I'm afraid there isn't. Not yet anyway," he said. He went on to say;"Since the scientists here at Duke found out the results of our study, research on cures for debilitating diseases such as Parkingson's, Lou Gehigs Disease, Cystic Fibrosis, Alzheimer's, and every type of cancer have been put on hold indefinitely. But a remedy will likely be a long time coming."

I suppose it's up to this reporter to offer some hope and encouragement for those who are lacking. So here it is:

Don't worry, men out there with teeny weenies; you'll be dead soon.

Madame Bitters

DORKING POST MODERN TRIANGULISTS GATHER AT FELCHERS BOTTOM

Followers of Dorking's thriving post-modernist Art society travelled to the Isle of Wight yesterday for their annual weekend get-together, writes **JPR Laidlaw, Dorking Review's Deputy Chief Rugby Football Correspondent**.

"Here we are once again on the dunes at Felchers Bottom," announced limestone sculptor and legendary Surrey Triangulist, Professor Roderick Chump-Parsnip, standing outside his own private tent.

"Greetings to all Dorking-based lovers of fine art, as we gather again to celebrate a weekend of the most innovative talent to be found anywhere throughout the Home Counties," he declared.

"Since my discovery of Dorking Triangulism in the 1070's our Society continues to stand alone against the tidal wave of post-war neo-romanticism," he explained. "Resisting those same forces of philistine artistic globalisation that have destroyed the soul of every British artist from William Hogarth to Damien Hurst."

"All art beyond Dorking is moribund. From Paris to Barcelona – from New York to Florence and from Shrewsbury to Leamington Spa," he declared.

"Remember that and you won't go far wrong."

"Children of Dorking. Immerse your brushes in the flow of divine inspiration. I hereby declare our 36th Annual Festival officially open!"

Several hours later, as the glorious sun began to dip below the horizon, I met up with Professor Chump-Parsnip for a gentle pre-dinner wander amongst the artists, clustered in small groups around the surrounding dunes.

"Felchers Bottom is where it's at," he whispered as we began our stroll.

"Look about, if you wish to savour the intoxicating aroma of the English Channel. Blending with the rapier-like thrust of Dorking paint brushes wielded by the children of Apollo."

"Have you seen Vernon Harding's 'Virgin and Child of Godalming'," he asked.

"Which one is Vernon Harding," I enquired.

"Surely you've heard of Vernon Harding," he replied sharply. "Runs the Kismet Oriental Grill at Mickleham. Couple of miles due north of Dorking town centre."

When I admitted I hadn't, the professor launched into an interesting account that compared Pablo Picasso unfavourably to Harding.

"Harding's work is everything that Pablo's isn't," he revealed.

"For one thing, Harding never uses blue."

"For another, Harding depicts the female breast, not as a geometric symbol but as a sacred farmyard animal. A fundamental breakthrough that would never have occurred to Picasso, a mere peasant from Malaga.

I then asked the professor to explain the artistic significance behind his own decision to sculpture rock only whilst completely naked.

"What is naked," he replied. "What is the human form? Other than a stroke of the brush. Or the strike of a sharp chisel."

Lady Catherine Versey-Palmiston then approached, clutching a newly completed canvas.

"What do you think Professor?"

"Ah! Nude Nymph With Dragon & Child," he replied. "It has form. Yes. And it has shape. Depicting the triumphant beast at rest over the fecund damsel. With a child, a subtle symbol of lost virginity. I particularly like your Dadaist montage of Dorking town square in the background. And your sensuous portrayal of a roaring River Mole in full flood, harking back to the Industrial Revolution."

"It is a triumph," he declared.

"Thanks only to you," quivered Lady Catherine. Who seemed not the least aware that she too was stark naked.

Later we walked across the dunes to pay courtesy visits on other leading artists.

Gabriella Fonsdyke and Brigitta Knatchbull from Brocketts Farm on the A246 near Polesden Lacey were roasting a brace of mallard by moonlight. Simultaneously, they were dropping ripe apples onto a pool of brilliant white emulsion.

"We are the niece of Henri Matisse," they chanted in unison.

"An erotic masterpiece on a theme of Sapphic resurrection," whispered Professor Chump-Parsnip as the two ladies continued their work. Oblivious to the gold oil paint smeared across their naked breasts.

"It's going to be "Venus & Diana In Paradise Beside Camilla's

Organic Grocery Shop in Leatherhead," he revealed as we crept away.

Tarquin Bickersdyke from Cathcart Road, West Horsley in Surrey is a distant cousin of Paul Gauguin.

"I've been following the Dorking School since I fell out with the Pre-Modiglianis," he said as he mixed us a Pimms.

"You won't find another movement like this anywhere."

"It's as if Leonardo da Vinci had met Banksy in Epsom and they'd moved into a Guildford squat with Velazquez and Tracy Emin."

"Right now, Dorking is the epicentre of World Art," he declared.

And on that note I left for a quiet pint at the Mason's Arms.

Juanita Juan

CHURCHILL'S SECRET SHAME REVEALED

Papers recently released by the government, reveal that Britain came close to losing the Second World War due to a fit of pique by the then prime minister Winston Churchill.

The papers show that in the spring of 1941 Churchill had received a telegram from President Roosevelt stating that the United Kingdom would have to pay the full market price for powdered egg imported from America.

Churchill was so upset by this that he went into one of the toilet cubicles in the Houses of Parliament and wrote '*Roosevelt is a cock sucking bastard*' on the inside of the door.

Fortunately, the next person to use the toilet was the Foreign Secretary, Lord Halifax, who during the course of evacuating his bowels noticed Churchill's distinctive hand writing. He immediately put an armed guard on the toilet cubicle to prevent any passing Americans from using it, and then went directly to Churchill's chambers to confront him with what he had discovered. Lord Halifax then insisted that Churchill be kept behind after the parliamentary session and made to clean the graffiti from all of the cubicles.

If word had got back to President Roosevelt, it would have been probable that the United States would not have entered the war, and just possible that they might have joined the other side, thus bankrupting Germany instead of Britain.

Historians are now combing the released papers for other unknown secret political/toilet incidents.

GM

UK's National Sperm Bank Privatised and Rebranded

Reacting to the shortage of sperm donors, the Government has announced that the UK's National Sperm Bank is to be put into 'private hands' and re-branded as 'The DOGGER BANK'.

In a bold initiative to tackle 'Wankrupt' UK, the new share-listed company will have commercial sponsorship and franchise link-ins from a major car park company. They promise to introduce 'innovative' methods of collecting sperm from willing donors.

"This is a private enterprise initiative, run along the same lines as any commercial bank. The board of the new company are all to a man, merchant bankers," enthuses CEO Michael Hunt.

"We've put traditional banking measures in place to attract interest from suitable males and the take-up has been overwhelming! They're coming in their thousands and we'll have to take on more staff to handle them all."

"At car park locations all over the country, our attractive cashiers will assist donors make speedy deposits and withdrawals. It's a 'hands-on' job, yet we've had thousands of applications so there's stiff competition for every available position. Armani have designed the staff uniform, complete with chic corporate boob-tube, jeggings and vajazzle." says Hunt.

"Also the public is very familiar with ATM, or 'Hole-in-the-wall' machines as they're known, and we're introducing similar devices into the car park toilets to enable 24-hour Sperm Banking. We call them 'Glory Holes-in the wall' and donors will be able to make deposits into them whenever and wherever they want willy-nilly."

"As for quality control, all donors will be CCTV'd which should open up...er, other financial opportunities for the company. We are determined to make massive profits from now on and we're not going to get palmed off, unlike our donors. On the shareholder side, we're hoping to avoid double dips on the stock-market, but positively encourage them in the car parks!"

A tumescent Hunt then posed with a few of his attractive cashiers for press photographers. "I hope they got their money shot," he wisecracked.

Before being whisked off, Hunt finished the Press Conference on a note of optimism: "Thanks to DOGGER BANK this country will have no shortage of sperm donors from now on. It should make a vast difference."

pinxit

ISLE OF WIGHT RESEARCH SENSATION

Top Isle of Wight people have welcomed academic research which has established the geographical nature of the holiday destination.

Research published by Ryde University yesterday proves that the island is completely surrounded by water.

"This is very exciting research," said Prof Newman Drumlin, head of the university's Earth Sciences department. "We began this programme five years ago to establish just exactly what made the Isle of Wight an island. We can confirm that it is because there is water around it everywhere. It's salt water – sea, in fact.

The next stage of the programme is to compare our data with other research institutions around the UK – we are in close touch with the Douglas Institute of Islands on the Isle of Man, for example. And who knows where it might lead on an international level? These are northern waters, so we're keen to make comparisons with warmer locations, like in the Mediterranean, or Indian Ocean."

The professor added that the high-powered research had cost a little over £15 million.

Editor of the Ryde and Newport Bugle, Phil "Scoop" Credible said: "This news is going to be welcomed by everyone here. It explains a lot – not least why we have to get a boat to go anywhere, or why tourists have to get on ferries or hovercraft to come here."

A senior member of the Cowes Sailing Club added: "I've suspected as much for years, but it's not the kind of thing you like to talk about – people think you're mad."

SM

DORKING ARTIST HAS EYE GRAFTED ONTO HIS PENIS

A performance artist who celebrates in shocking his audience has had a third eye surgically constructed onto his penis.

'Wanksy', real name Sid Wanksy, focuses his work on extending the capabilities of the human body. The controversial artist has already undergone two complicated surgeries to implant the art-in-progress on the end of his member after struggling for months to find a surgeon willing to perform the contentious technique.

And his next idea is to install a small webcam in the extra eye, so his audience can tune in and see what his penis is 'up to'.

Wanksy, 60, said: "The eye is part of a process – a conceptual raisin d' etre. It is a permanent part of me now, as after six months it became fused to my willy, with its own blood supply."

"The final procedure will re-implant a miniature webcam to enable a wireless connection to the internet, making it a remote Skype device for people in other places. For example, someone in Bratislava could see what my penis can see in Dorking. Whether it be nestled comfortably in my boxer shorts or, say, looking at the ducks and up into the sky in the local park."

"This project has been about replicating a bodily structure, relocating it and re-wiring it to better function in the technological and media terrain we now inhabit."

Agnes Beecham, from Dorking's Over 60's Watercolour Club, is part of the team involved in bringing Wanksy's work to the local Arts Centre. She said: "Mr Wanksy's installation aims to connect people through technology and social networking sites such as YouTube, and this is simply a more extreme extension of that. Only this morning, Sid's eye winked and gave me a poke on Facebook."

"His work seems frivolous, but it does raise some serious issues surrounding the body, technology, perception and mental health. I guess you could say it brings a 21st century artistic take on the 'one-eyed trouser snake'."

pinxit

FORBIDDEN TITTY FOUND IN FORBIDDEN CITY

Beijing – A team of Russian Archaeologists working on excavations in one of China's Forbidden Cities have stumbled across a discovery, more astounding than the Terracotta Army.

The terracotta soldiers, it will be remembered, represented the Army of the Emperor Qin to accompany him into the afterlife, and were found in Xi'an in Shaanxi province China during the boring of a well by local farmers.

Last month, a group of Russian archaeologists led by Olga-Maria Dygomupski of the Lenin-Lumumba Institute in Novosibirsk were carrying out routine dendro-dating of the wood in various shrines in the Sha Giu region of Shaanxi when they got more than they bargained for.

Hidden mine subsides

Explains Ms Dygomupski: "Ve voss drilling vooden core sample in da flooring of shrine, ven suddenly great crack appear (in more vays than ve imagining vere) and ve fall through into great dark hole beneath. Lucky no vun voss hurt except teknician Yuri Bolackov who all times scream anyvay ven lights go out, like he being buggered by Cossack against lamp post in back-alley in Minsk. He only broke fingernail, blooding great voman. I strike match see vere ve are and then I see marvellous sight, row upon row of glistening porcelaine figures of vomans!"

What Olga-Maria and her group had stumbled upon was a whole array of porcelaine female figures each 1.67526m high, arranged in rows in a long underground room lined with wood. On further removal of the overburden and exposure to the light which took another week's work, she then realised that Emperor Qin had not only expected to take his whole army with him but also his wives and concubines. Mining activities had caused ground weaknesses in the area and these are thought to have resulted in the serendipitous discovery. The sight that met Olga's eyes was astounding.

China wives and concubines

"Some of vomens voss fully clothed and had frowns and scowls and sticking out the tongues voss; very ugly vomens, look like bad shit in latrine after hot stroganov. These I thinking am voss the vives of Great Emperor Qin.

"The udder vomens was in different undressings, had pouty lipses long eyelash and beckoning vere their fingers, stiff and solid like Moscow hooker in doorway on frosty night, these his concubines vere.

"Some completely nakeds vere, every contour of body, every fold of skin, even waginas perfect; breasts like domes on Kremlin, like Miss Russia slut in HD porn film on imported Japaneses telewision in seedy flat in concrete apartment block in Vladivostok. Typical blooding man these voss his special fawourites I suppose."

"Some of figures voss wery dangerous; ve find bones of past raiders vith severed fingers stuck in wagina holeses of figures because of special mechanism inside hollow bodies." said Ms Dygomupski.

Dating of the figures has been done by Academician Denis Ivanovitch at the Institute of Archaeology, now housed in the buildings of the old Lubyanka Prison in Gotno Prospekt, Moscow. And the figures have definitely been placed at around 200-250 BC.

However, foreseeing the possibility of tomb raiders, the Emperor Qin had booby trapped some of the figures, and Olga-Maria came across some chilling sights.

Real Booby Traps

"Some of figures voss wery dangerous; ve find bones of past raiders vis severed fingers stuck in wagina holeses of figures because of special mechanism inside hollow bodies. Some ven touched launched knifeses, vich burst out of breastses, due to wery sensitive tilt detection, real booby traipses eh! Chinese translator fellow, he have narrow escape. He already got cock out in hand near prettiest of figures. He look like Elephant vith hepatitis in Moscow zoo; if teknician Yuri not have screamed ve never be able to order taxi back to hotel again because nobody speak the Chinese talkings like him."

No doubt there will be more discoveries, since it is expected that the Emperor would have provided camp-followers for his troops also. In order to raise money for excavations, part of the finds will be on tour around the world next year. The exhibition will be visiting Britain at the following venues:

London – British Museum: 6-23 June "Kings and Concubines, Qing Dynasty Female Figures 240 BC."

Manchester Museum: December "King-pin Qin's Quim: Ming Minge from the China Vagina Mine."

This story first appeared in the November issue of the National Geographic Educational Supplement, and the full story of the translator's narrow escape is due to appear in *Chinks in Heat* Magazine under the title: "Cunning Linguist Fla Tjio, Narrowly Escapes Cock Chop Suey by Emperor's China Doll.

LC

NOBEL COMMITTEE HAILS LIGHTYEAR AS 'EINSTEIN' OF 21ST CENTURY'

In a move that delighted scientists around the world, Dr Buzzard M Lightyear III of Pixar Corp was today awarded the Nobel Prize for Physics.

The citation reads:
The Norwegian Nobel Committee has decided that the Nobel Prize for Physics is to be awarded to Dr Lightyear for his outstanding achievement in Quantum physics and Mathematics. The Committee has attached special importance to his ingeniously simple hypothesis, 'To infinity and beyond', in which he has overturned conventional quantum and maths theory and imparted a new world vision and hope to mankind, immortality and whatever 'stuff' lies beyond.

It is a ground-breaking paradigm; that there is something longer than Sisyphean infinity. With this giant leap, he has boldly gone beyond contemporary quantum theory of 'strings', as he clearly doesn't need any. His work will go on forever and a day, and possibly a day after that.

Accepting his prize, Dr Lightyear, 15, issued a brief statement. "I feel humbled. My eternal and a bit further thanks go to my Dad, the evil Emperor Zurg, without whom I wouldn't be here. I've simply been standing on the shoulders of giants like Aristotle, Newton,

Einstein and Mr Potato-Head."

The Nobel Prize winner is due to deliver his Nobel Lecture in Stockholm in October, batteries permitting.

pinxit

NOSTALGIA ON THE WANE AS OLD PEOPLE FORGET WHAT THEY WERE GETTING NOSTALGIC ABOUT

If you are fortunate enough to be able to recall when this country last had a Labour government, Dorking were a successful football team, and beer was only £3.00 a pint, then you're probably one of the dying breed of individuals afflicted with *nostalgia.*

Nostalgia – the act of fond remembrance of times gone by, is dying out faster than rainforests and corner shops, according to nostalgia expert Dr Yaroslav Yesterdayev of Krakow College of Rusty Bolt Loosening.

"It's the old folks," he told us. "They get to a point where they forget what they were getting nostalgic about. And then they get all cranky and frustrated because they've forgotten how it feels to feel good. That's when the temper tantrums start up. They'll be grumpy and irritable. They have been known to throw dinner plates on the floor and even bite people. Usually on the hand, where it really hurts. Especially if they've got their dentures in."

Further research has proved beyond any doubt that Dr Yesterdayev is correct in his findings, with an added twenty-first century twist – modern old people refuse to accept that they are getting old. So as such, they don't feel nostalgic, they feel like years ago was this morning, and this morning was when Abba topped the charts. They don't see their 'wobbly bits' or the grey hair, or the baldness, and they still think their kids are spoilt brats. Even when their 'kids' are 44 years old.

"It's a lost generation," Dr Yesterdayev said sadly. "This generation can't comprehend how Debbie Harry turned into a little old lady, where Joanna Lumley's wrinkles came from, or why 'young' 40 year old footballers can't run at 150 mph any more, and are starting to go a bit bald. This is the first generation in the history of humanity that thinks it hasn't changed. Sad bastards..."

Ah yes. I remember it well.... Bits of it.

Skoob 1999

DISCOVERY OF SHAKESPEARE FIRST DRAFT SUGGESTS HE 'MAY HAVE BEEN GAY'

First x-ray pictures of William Shakespeare's newly uncovered jottings for what is probably his most famous and popular sonnet were unveiled today at Oxford's Bodleian Library. And according to Professor Benjamin Grimwade they're 'dynamite'.

Sonnet 18 – as it is known to academics, begins; 'Shall I compare thee to a summer's day? ' and includes the classic phrase 'Darling buds of May'. It is the best known of all the Bard's 154 sonnets and has always been thought of as a love poem to a fair maid with whom the young Will was besotted.

However, the scribbled, crossed out, erased and amended first thoughts of Shakespeare show the poem in a very different light. It may have been originally addressed to a burly Stratford-upon-Avon bricklayer.

"The references to *'codpiece jeggings'*, *'thy rippling lallies'*, *darling plums of May'* and *'lay thine quivering dabber in mine hardcore fundaments'* are open to interpretation" says Professor Grimwade, "But his original first line *'Shall I compare thee to a bummer's gaye?'* is pretty unequivocal.

pinxit

THIS IS THE STORY OF A MARRIAGE. AS REVEALED THROUGH THE SEPARATE CORRESPONDENCE OF A LOVING HUSBAND AND WIFE.

Brenda Stoat has a ten-a-day letter writing habit and can usually be found sitting at her dining room table in 37 Acacia Drive Dorking, complaining about something or other. Meanwhile, upstairs in the back bedroom, her husband Ronald is doing exactly the same on his laptop:-

Sir,

I am moved to complain most seriously about your vile monthly periodical 'The Complete Spanker' delivered to this household in error today via brown envelope. Imagine my shock to discover a private snap of myself, taken 30 years ago, included in the disgusting article you call 'Reader's Wives."

Yours angrily,
Brenda Stoat (Mrs)

Dear Lord Big Balls,

Let me congratulate you on your excellent ancient history feature 'Reader's Wives'. And thank you for including my modest contribution. I am in receipt of your cheque for £50.00 and look forward to next month's powerful modern history feature. I feel the 'Complete Spanker' provides a valuable service to our quiet suburban community.

Sincerely,
Ron Stoat (62)

Dear Mrs Pomfroy,

Please find enclosed our cheque for £25 as deposit for a two week stay on your caravan site in the isolated woodlands of Flenwynthllgollen in North Wales. This is the sort of holiday my husband and I look forward to. Total peace and quiet with just ourselves for company. Perfect bliss! We shall arrive on Tuesday fortnight.

Yours gratefully
Mrs Brenda Stoat.

Dear Sir,

With reference to your advertisement for striptease artists in 'Totally Thai Tits'. I am a 62 year old retired decorator (references available) and active supporter of local wildlife. That said, I am currently seeking a new challenge and wonder if you have openings for experienced wardrobe staff in Bangkok. I am a single gentleman, prepared to relocate.

Sincerely,
Ron Stoat.

Dear Sir,

May I draw your attention to the recent epidemic of sex offences in the Dorking area. I believe this has much to do with the so-called clothing commonly worn by young women locally. When will they realise that drawing attention to themselves with items such as lipstick, visible brassiere straps and the occasional showing of flimsy undergarments, merely converts them into targets for inappropriate advances. Despite leading an active life in every respect, I have never been bothered by perverts.

Yours ever,
Brenda Stoat (Mrs)

Dear Madam,

May I politely ask if there are any vacancies within your underwear department. As you are surely aware, many women select their underwear with a gentleman in mind. So perhaps some customers would welcome the honest opinion of an experienced Lingerie Selection Consultant such as myself.

Yours respectably,
Ronald P Stoat.

Dear Sir,

I write to complain about your recent marketing campaign which I deem aggressive beyond belief. What on earth made you imagine my husband Ronald would be in the least interested in sampling three pairs of leather thongs from your new 'Naughty Lucy' range?
I return them forthwith at your expense and trust you will learn your lesson.

Yours in exasperation
Brenda Stoat (Mrs)

Dear Sir,

I wish to register a complaint about breast feeding facilities in the Dorking branch of your supermarket chain. Why have you now confined these natural activities to your new Mother & Baby Suite? Frankly I miss the heartening sight of young mothers feeding their babies on the chairs on Aisle 9 (by the checkout tills). There's nothing rude about breast feeding in public.

Yours
Ron Stoat.

Sir,

I wish to complain about your database. Why on earth do you presume to send your filthy periodical 'Totally Thai Tits' to number 37 Acacia Drive under cover of a plain brown envelope? Can't you understand there's nobody living here remotely interested in such vile pornography. Suppose my husband, Ronald, were to come across it! Kindly strike us off your list with immediate effect.

Brenda Stoat (Mrs)

Dear Sir,

I write to say how informative I found your article about Russian women seeking true love with men from the west. This is the sort of work our Ministry For Overseas Development should be doing. With reference to your list. May I draw your attention to 19 year old Oxana (blond bombshell on page 96 column 5 second from the left). I believe we are ideally matched and would be obliged if you would forward her my full details, currently held on record.

Yours faithfully,
Ron Stoat.

Dear Dr Mould,

I write with bad news. Those pills you gave me have had little or no effect. My flushes have failed to subside. Even worse, the snakes I told you about are now appearing whenever I shut my eyes. Furthermore, I am starting to dream of telegraph poles and poplar trees. I can't take much more and am afraid I might eventually submit to the inevitable. Is it possible to increase the dose?

Yours gratefully,
Mrs Brenda Stoat.

Dear Sir,

What became of the leather thongs I ordered from your 'Naughty Lucy' range? Please forward them without further delay. On a separate issue, I too sympathise with the tribal people of the Andaman Islands. I found your article most informative. Particularly the photographs of naked females cleaning themselves in the river. The way extremely young girls mixed freely with older women was an astonishing revelation. Could we have lots more of this sort of thing?

Yours faithfully,
Ron Stoat.

Dear Father Brown,

I'm sure my husband, Ronald, would be delighted to volunteer for bell-ringing lessons every Monday night until further notice. He'll be free to start next week.

Yours always
Mrs Brenda Stoat.

Dear Mrs Lubbock,

Please consider me for the vacant position of Female Shower Attendant at Dorking Swimming Baths. As an elderly married man of limited vision and no interest whatsoever in young ladies, I am an ideal candidate. I believe local girls would soon come to look upon me as a father figure. May I suggest I come for a trial session at 3.00 pm next Wednesday.

Yours sincerely,
Ronald P Stoat Esq.

Sir,

I am not a complaining sort of person. But this time the Postage Department of your Company has gone too far. A junior clerk within your organisation still insists on sending a monthly copy of 'Private Wives' to this address. In spite of my 40 minute telephone conversation of Friday last, when I assured the kind gentleman that my name was not Dora from Devon. Please now strike 37 Acacia Drive Dorking from the computer database of both Private Wives and 'Bosom Buddies'.

Yours,
Brenda Stoat (Mrs)

Dear Headmistress,

In respect of your advertisement for a Gym Instructor at St Mary's Convent School. I wonder if you would consider an all-rounder. I am an experienced Olympic Games coach who once prepared the Cambodian Ladies Indoor Volleyball team. I also specialise in everything to do with the swimming pool. Particularly the breast stroke, in which my hands-on teaching methods have been recognised around the world. I'm confident your girls would soon appreciate having me around.

Yours faithfully,
Ronald P Stoat

Dear Lord Big Balls,

Following last month's outrage, why on earth have you sent me yet another edition of your vile periodical 'The Compete Spanker'? It is now on the fire together with your invoice. You are a despicable person and a disgrace to the House of Lords.

Yours etc
Brenda Stoat (Mrs)

Dear Big Don,

Where is my copy of this month's issue of 'Private Wives'? My annual subscription of £52.99 was paid on June the first as requested. Please check account of Dora from Devon and supply me with such back issues you have neglected to send.

Yours in confidence,
Ron Stoat.

Dear Sir,

As Executive Producer of the Nine o'clock news, may I implore you to have a quiet word with every one of your female newscasters. Without exception nowadays, they find occasion to lean forward and expose the upper part of their chest. Whilst others have picked up the unseemly habit of continually crossing and uncrossing their legs, drawing attention to that most sensitive area of their anatomy. Things got so bad last night, I was forced to switch off and send my husband, Ronald , out to make tea!

Yours sincerely,
Brenda Stoat (Mrs)

Dear TV Boss,

I wish to complain about newscaster Kate Silverton who does not answer my mail. As an employee of the BBC, I am prepared to accept that she will never show me her breasts live on air. However, I have written to her privately on numerous occasions, enclosing a photograph of another woman's breasts which I believe to be similar in every respect. All I request is a simple yes or no answer that my theory is correct. Is that too much to ask?

Yours sincerely,
Ron Stoat (62)

Dear Sir,

May I confirm that my husband, Ronald, and myself will be happy to attend your clinic next Wednesday at 11.00 am to donate blood. Neither of us takes sugar with our tea and we are not fussy about biscuits. Two shortbread or digestives will suffice.

Yours sincerely,
Brenda Stoat (Mrs)

Dear Sir,

Further to your advertisement in this week's Dorking Review, may I offer to donate sperm. I'll see you next Tuesday afternoon when you'll be welcome to as much as your nurse can get. Might I request Nurse Karen who I noticed when I checked you out. Or perhaps Sister Denise who looks to have a promising career within the local NHS.

Yours sincerely,
Ron Stoat (62)

Dear Dr Clackett,

I was planning to take my husband, Ronald on a hill-walking holiday this autumn. Possibly in Yorkshire. Or maybe North Wales. However, he now tells me that you have strictly forbidden him to walk further than half a mile at a stretch. Furthermore, he now claims you have advised him to take a complete rest by himself on a beach somewhere in South East Asia. Might I ask you to arrange for a second opinion on all this.

Yours sincerely,
Brenda Stoat (Mrs).

Dear Nature Lovers,

Further to your advertisement in this month's 'As Nature Intended', I wish to confirm that I'm keen to have a go. My wife and I haven't booked a holiday for this summer so we are definitely up for it. Brenda is an avid bird-watcher. Could you send her a list of what birds she might expect to see at your colony. In a separate brown envelope, could you send me photographic evidence of other sights I might expect to encounter. You know the sort of thing: Pictures of your guests playing volleyball. Or leaning over a barbecue.

Yours sincerely,
Ron Stoat (62).

Juanita Juan

IRISH DANCE WORLD SHOCK

The world of Irish folk dancing has been thrown into turmoil following the discovery of an ancient text. The discovery was made by historian Declan O'Handcream while carrying out research at Trinity College, Dublin. Searching through some ancient books in a rarely-visited section of the college library, he came across a dusty old tome which looked like it hadn't been opened in years.

Imagine his surprise when, on blowing away the dust and cobwebs, he saw the title: "The Irish Dance, Part Two: The arms."

"Well you could have knocked me down with a feather for sure," said Dr O'Handcream. "As a historian, you always hope to discover an unknown text that will throw light on some aspect of history. But to find something as culturally significant as this is amazing!"

Irish dance experts are now examining the 500-odd page book, which is beautifully illuminated in bright coloured inks and gold leaf.

(With acknowledgements to cartoonist Ed McLachlan)

Dance critic, Neville "Leapy" Points, said: "This is sooooo exciting, and offers a simply super opportunity for the likes of Michael Flatley to reinvent their shows. We can all enjoy *Riverdance* all over again – with arms! How wonderful, love!"

SM

OSCAR WILDE WASN'T GAY

New evidence emerged last week proving that the writer Oscar Wilde was not gay, as was previously thought.

A diary belonging to one of Wilde's associates – The Marquis of Tewkesbury, shows an entry for the summer of 1898 when the Marquis and his companions were spending a weekend with Wilde at Eastbourne.

Splendid fun today. General Butler hired two bathing machines. One for the men, and one for the ladies in order that we could all benefit from an immersion in the sea. Porters were employed to haul the machines into the water, and much hilarity was to be had when Mrs Pilkington-Wright was heard to declare that should she continue in the fashion of a duck she would be likely to grow feathers. Everyone had an extremely gay time except for Oscar Wilde who refused to join in, and spent the day in a public house – The miserable bastard!

The literary world has been rocked by this new evidence of Oscar Wilde's un-gayness, and it is thought that many of the books celebrating his life will now have to be rewritten.

Wilde's latest biographer, Dave Bathplug from Chelmsford said: "I am totally shocked to learn that Oscar Wilde wasn't gay. It's well documented that he had anal sex with other men, and you would have thought that anyone who allows another bloke to do that to you must have had a sense of humour."

GM

MASTURBATION
'BIGGEST FACTOR' IN ELVIS-STYLE FATALITIES

Self-abuse, coffee, blowing your nose and straining to defecate could increase the risk of a fatal stroke similar to Elvis Presley's, say researchers in Madrid.

Eight risk factors were linked to bleeding on the brain. They all increase blood pressure which could result in aneurysms (blood vessels bursting), according to research published in the journal 'Diferentes Estilos' (Different Strokes).

"Masturbation is the riskiest activity, but a combination of habits done simultaneously or in close proximity make early death almost inevitable," says research head Professore al médico Juan Kerr.

"If an obese middle-aged man drinks a double espresso vodka chaser while simultaneously straining to defecate, smoking a cigarette, blowing his nose, coughing and masturbating on the toilet, then his chances of incurring a fatal infarction rise by 5,000%."

"Fortunately, there are not too many men who can multi-task like that, hence the relatively low incidence of mortality from such an incident." says Prof Kerr.

"Elvis was the exception that proved the rule."

pinxit

MADAME BITTERS PROBLEM PAGE

Dear Madame Bitters,

I have had a weight problem my whole life and right now I'm the heaviest I've ever been. I've tried dieting and exercising, but the pounds won't budge. Please help me, I'm desperate.

Fat and Frustrated.

Fat and Frustrated:

Normally I don't answer questions about diet and weight related issues, and it's not because I don't know what I'm talking about. I'm well into my 40s and I have maintained the sylph-like figure I've had since I was a teenager. I don't answer dieting questions because it's simply beneath me and it wastes my time when I could be helping others with real problems.

But, since you said you were desperate, I suppose I can break my rile this one time. Here are the methods I use to keep trim and not one of them involves 'eating right' or going to the gym:

*I smoke. I smoke more than a fourteen year old runway model does. I smoke because it keeps my weight down and because it just looks cool. I prefer menthols but any kind will do.

Do try to stay away from Ultra-Lites though. It's like sucking on a straw and since they contain less nicotine & tobacco, the desired outcome is muted. Don't waste your time on them.

*I drink. I drink so much that my liver is probably the size of a cantaloupe. Everyone says that alcohol is fattening – those people are liars.

Booze doesn't have any fat in it, but it does have a lot of calories. What they don't tell you is that after you've downed 6 gin and tonics in less than an hour, the last thing you want to do is eat. In fact, you'll probably vomit and we all know that if your lunch is in the toilet it definitely won't settle on your hips, will it? Just be careful with mixers like coke, juice etc. You don't want to dilute alcohol's weight loss magic.

On average I drink about 14-15 drinks a day, about 9 of which are vodka martinis. I like martinis because when I drink them I feel sophisticated. I also drink Scotch, neat and just to mix it up a bit I also drink absinthe on occasion. I doubt you'll be able to drink that much right now. It took me years, but if you really want to be thin you'll find a way.

*I snort a lot of cocaine. It's my favourite no-calorie sweetener. I've been doing it for years and besides the occasional 3-day-long nosebleed, it's never done me any harm.

I do have one word of caution: If the thought of serving a prison sentence for possession scares you, or if you already have 2 strikes, I strongly suggest you not to do this.

On another note, prison actually isn't too bad. It's where I learned how to do origami and it gave me time to hone my writing skills. It's also a great environment for sexual experimentation – way better than college ever was.

If these tips don't produce the results you want there is one other option:

*Contact e.coli or salmonella. Really, any sort of food-borne illness or intestinal parasite will do it. All you have to do is eat undercooked, spoiled food or visit a third world country and drink their water. It's as easy as that. I sometimes do this when I feel particularly bloated or puffy, and it works every time.

Those are my 4 foolproof ways to lose weight. If you follow them and you don't die, you'll look fabulous. However, in the interest of safety I must advise you that before starting this or any weight loss regime, please check with your healthcare provider. If your doctor gives you the go ahead, you need to find a new doctor.

Madame Bitters.

Dear Madame Bitters,

I'm a single woman well into my 30s and I'm more than ready to settle down. I'm dating a man who is sweet and considerate, but he's a loser in every other sense. He's a garbage man, he's 50lbs overweight and a horrible dresser. He goes to comic book and sci-fi conventions and he says "Okie dokie" way, way too much. He's crazy about me and he wants to make a life with me. I hate to say it, but I know I'm too good for this person, and I know I deserve better. What do you think?

Conflicted.

Conflicted:

Your situation reminds me of a song that I can't remember the name of. Luckily for you I do remember the chorus. Here it is:

If you want to be happy for the rest of your life
Never make a pretty woman your wife
So from my personal point of view

Get an ugly girl to marry you.

There's also a line about the singer not caring if the girl's 'eyes don't match' in there someplace and it always makes me chuckle.
The lesson you should take from this song is that the uglier and less desirable your mate is the better your chances are of them worshipping the ground you walk on. They'll be loyal to you like a toothless, crippled dog.

Another bonus of being with someone who's beneath you is this person likely has no self esteem. Ugly people always know they are ugly. Therefore, your guy knows that you're too good for him. He will bend over backwards to keep you happy and in his life. Use this fact to your advantage and feel free to walk all over him like cheap threadbare shag carpeting.

From the tone of your letter you sound like the type of snotty bitch who would enjoy breaking a decent man's spirit for the purpose of playing to your own vanity. So go nuts.

Madame Bitters.

PS: You said you were "well into" your 30s, so I'm going to assume that you're turning 40 next week. At your age you need to grab onto the first willing guy and drag him down the aisle if necessary. On the bright side, sometimes wives accidentally throw their wedding & engagement rings in the garbage bin. If you choose to stay with this guy you might get a nice ring out of it.

Dear Madame Bitters,

Yesterday, when I came home from work early, I got the shock of my life. I walked in on 'Stan' my husband of 8 years dressed up in women's clothing, some of which were mine. He was even wearing lingerie, heels and make-up! Stan swears to me he isn't gay and that he dresses in women's clothing to 'unwind' He also confessed he's been doing it since he was a teenager. I don't think he's gay, but I just don't understand why he feels the need to dress in drag. What do you think?

Feeling Deceived

Feeling Deceived:

I think you weren't paying attention when your husband told you why he dresses in drag. He said he did it to unwind. I mean come on, I wasn't even there when this whole Jerry Springer-esque scene unfolded, but I *was* paying attention when I read your letter.
However, I can appreciate how jarring it must have been for you to walk in on your husband and find him dressed up like an extra from *The Crying Game*, so I'll forgive you for your poor listening skills. Just don't make a habit of it.

Madame Bitters thinks you are looking at the situation between Stan and yourself the wrong way. If you've read my column before, you know that I'm no Polyanna glad-game playing optimist. However, you also know that if there's any way I can turn a bad situation to my (or in this case, your) advantage I'll find it.
In your letter you said some of the clothes you caught Stan wearing were yours. Don't you see how great that is? If you and your husband wear the same size, you can double your wardrobe, girlfriend.

If the two of you go shopping together he'll actually be able to give you helpful answers to questions you may ask, like: "Do these boots look slutty to you?" and "Does this skirt make my ass look big?" Your soul mate is also a great shopping partner. Do you realize how lucky you are?

You also mentioned that your husband was wearing makeup. You may not know this, but cross dressers and drag queens always have *the* best cosmetics. I'm talking MAC, Smashbox, and the high priced, good quality stuff. So take advantage of this and raid his makeup drawer ASAP.

These are just two of the vast, vast number of possibilities you have now that you know your husband is a cross dresser. And since he's not gay, what's the problem?

Here's what Madame Bitters suggests: Next Saturday night you and your husband put on your hottest dresses, get dolled up, and hit the clubs together. If drinking together, clubbing together, and being able to share your husband's lipstick don't constitute the perfect union then what the fuck good is it?

Dear Madame Bitters,

My husband 'Terry' and I separated in early May of this year after fourteen years of marriage, and our divorce was finalized last week. While I'm relieved that Terry and I are no longer married, I was with him for a good chunk of my life, and I'm just not used to being alone. I'm only 34 and I feel like I'm at a crossroads in my life. How can I deal with it?

Flummoxed.

Flummoxed:

Let me tell you something about divorce: You can only feel one of two ways about it. You can be emotionally shattered about it, or you can feel like you've just had a 200 pound life-draining, dream-smashing, gas-passing tumor removed. Madame Bitters speaks with authority on the subject of failed marriages because she has been divorced three times.

I've actually been married five times, but I've been widowed twice. I've been advised by my team of lawyers not to discuss the events surrounding the deaths of two of my husbands, as the police are still conducting their investigation.

The point I'm trying to make is that since I've been divorced more times than I've been widowed, you've asked the right person for advice.

I just told you that there were two schools of thought on divorce; emotional devastation and relief.

It sounds like you identify with the second group which is good for both of us. Because there's no way I'm going to listen to you bitch and moan about how much you miss your husband and how you, "let him slip away." It's no secret that I hate whiners and that I refuse to coddle crybabies. So let's press on, shall we?

I suggest the first thing you do is throw yourself a 'Divorce shower'. Tie tin cans to the bumper of your car and write 'Just Divorced' on the back window in shoe polish. With the money you got from the divorce settlement (you have better gotten at least six-figures, or Madame Bitters will be *very* disappointed in you) go and celebrate your new-found freedom in style.

Go to the store and take your platinum credit card with you. After you've got the party refreshments, book yourself a few male strippers. Look under the "Adult Entertainment" section of the phone book if you're unsure where to start.

Invite all of your friends (including friends that both you and your ex-husband share) and party until you forget why you threw the party in the first place. Terry? Who's that?

If your ex-husband crashes your bash, take this opportunity to provide the other party-goers with a bit of unscheduled entertainment. Chances are he's going to be upset when he finds out how well you're doing after the divorce and how you aren't curled up in a foetal position pining away for him. When he gets there, tell him how much you're enjoying life without him and wait for him to come unglued. This is the sort of unscripted entertainment that party goers enjoy most, aside from the strippers that is.

You may be wondering what to do once the party has ended, but who says it has to? You were married all through your twenties, which is the decade when adults are supposed to experience life to its fullest. You're 34 now, so you've got to make up for lost time.
Get a tattoo, get something pierced, get a job in the sex industry, do anything you couldn't do when you were married. In short **get a life!!!** This is an order, and you don't want to disobey Madame Bitters. Just ask my former husbands, or the ones that are still alive anyway.

Dear Madame Bitters,

I'm 63 and the proud grandmother of three wonderful grandchildren. 'Kaleb', is five and twins 'Karmen' and Kasey' are four. Their father, 'Steve' is my son. Steve and my daughter in law both work full time and I take care of my grandchildren while they work. One of them drops the kids off at 8am and one of them picks the kids up around 6pm. This is the routine Monday-Friday. Now, I love my grandkids, but they're running me ragged. They bounce off the walls and are always into everything. They're good, sweet kids but they're driving me crazy. I know I shouldn't feel this way about my own grandchildren, but I do. What can I do to cope?

Overwhelmed Grandma.

Overwhelmed Grandma:

If there's one thing that brings joy into the heart of Madame Bitters it's the sound of happy children playing **-except when they're playing in front of my home when I'm trying to sleep it off.** At those times I wish I had a 17th century well in my backyard that I could throw those kids down. But I digress.

Your son and daughter in law are inconsiderate clods, but they're certainly not stupid. They know a good thing when they find it and that's free childcare from the best relative for the job; Grandma.

You see, your son is under the impression that since he grew up and left home you must be lonely and need someone to take care of; someone to break your stuff and a reason for you to consider buying a firearm. A replacement, if you will.

Lucky for you he and his wife have given you three 'replacements', and it sounds like they're doing a fine job of making you nuts. Steve thinks you're bored and that you're grateful for the 50 hour a week distraction. We both know better, don't we?

You can do one of two things. You could stand up to your son and his better half and tell them that you refuse to be taken advantage of anymore. Tell them that you've got your own life to live and it doesn't involve hyperactive, spastic grandkids. However, since we both know you're a spineless jellyfish or things wouldn't have gotten to this point, let's explore the second option.

Run your grandkids as ragged as they've ran you. Take them to the park, playground or public pool if the weather cooperates. It doesn't matter so much where you take them as long as it's a place where they can run, shout and wear themselves out. It may take hours for them to do this, so make sure to bring a book.

If you need something that's physically demanding done around your house, tell the grandkids how much fun it is. For instance, if you're planning to install a new septic tank, have the grandkids dig the hole. You wouldn't need to do much convincing because kids love to dig holes. Just use your imagination to make any hard labour seem like a 'game'.

What about if the weather's too bad to go outside? That's easy: drug them. When it's time for their cookies and juice, feel free to mix in a bit of vodka for a 'kiddy screwdriver'. When they eat pudding or yoghurt, add some crushed up Benedryl to it. In less than twenty minutes they'll be fast asleep face down in the tapioca.

It makes no difference if it's Nyquil or Robitussin, tequila or bourbon, Valium or Ambien, the results should be the same: blessed silence. While they're passed out like little winos, feel free to take a nice relaxing bubble bath. You've earned it.

Dear Madame Bitters,

I've had my job for a little over 3 years and I haven't been promoted yet. I work hard on my projects and I do a good job, but nothing's come of it. In fact, I've trained two people below me and they've already been moved up. I'm getting very discouraged and I'm thinking about quitting. What do you think I should do?

Depressed.

Depressed:

I've got to be honest with you; I've never held a 'job' in the technical sense for longer than a month or two, so kudos to you for your determination. That being said, I think it's time for you to quit your job.

I know my advice goes against the don't-give-up, never-say-die attitude that's prevalent in society today, but I don't care. I'm right and society is wrong.

Me: 1 / Society: 0

Let me expand on this: If something is hard to do, it's rarely worth doing. If you're staring in the face of adversity, just throw up your hands, say, "Fuck that shit," and go get yourself a pitcher of frozen margaritas. I don't know about you, but my time is too valuable to waste on tedious tasks.

So cut your losses and quit. Just tell your idiot boss you're going for a coffee run and leave. Before you go, make sure you grab all the free office supply swag you can stuff in your pockets and orifices.

Of course, you'll need to find employment eventually. When you do land a new job, you need to reprogram yourself to work in a new way. Here are a few hints for workplace success:

*Kick butt during your first 3 to 6 months at your new job. This is how long most companies have for new employees' probation.

If the company that hires you doesn't have a probation period for new employees, disregard this first step.

*Assuming you've lasted the first few months, we can proceed to step two which is to agree with, and suck up to your superiors. Ideally, you want to start this process during the interview by asking intelligent questions and then nodding thoughtfully. From that point you want to start kissing up slowly but steadily. The key is to pace yourself or you'll end up looking like Eddie Haskill, which is not the goal here. The more you suck up to your superiors, the more you can slack off when they're not looking.

*Continue to slack off.

*Surround yourself with smart, innovative employees. You may not have a speck of talent or charisma, but if you're part of a group who is, you'll be guilty by association.
After you ingratiate yourself with the right people, watch them. Pretend you're studying chimpanzees in the wilds of Africa. Notice how they interact with the higher-ups in the company. Scrutinize

them for weaknesses. Start a dossier on each one if you like.

*Keep slacking off, slacker.

*Keep your ear close to the office grapevine. If someone's getting fired, you want to know so you can manoeuvre yourself into the vacant spot. If you're the one getting fired, you need to find out quickly so you can find someone to blame. So get in with the office busybodies. Knowledge is power that you can use against your enemies.

If this sounds a tad ruthless that's because it is. It's a deadly serious business. The armed forces have basic training for warfare. This is your primer, your 'basic training' on the intricacies of office warfare. Follow them and you'll succeed and become CEO. Disregard them and you'll fail and end up as a POW in the mailroom. The choice is yours. Just don't say you weren't warned.

Dear Madame Bitters,

I'm so upset with my twin brother and my girlfriend that I just don't know what to do. "Staci" and I have been going out together since school, and she's the only girl I've ever loved. We're both 20 now and lately we've been talking about marriage. I thought everything was fine, but three days ago she told me that she and my twin brother "Keith" have been sleeping together the entire time Staci and I have been together. Now Staci and Keith are going out. The two people I'm closest to in the world have betrayed me – with each other. What should I do?

Heartbroken.

Heartbroken:

It's never too early to learn the bitter disappointment associated with love and Family. It will likely be a long time before you'll be able to trust anyone again. You've been hurt and this is to be expected. Do you know what might help you feel better though?

Revenge sex.

Staci needs to be taught a lesson (don't worry, we'll get to your brother in a bit) that she will never, ever forget.
You're going to have to fuck Staci's mum.

You may be asking yourself, *why does it have to be her mother; why not her sister, friend, or cousin?* I'll tell you why, smart guy: Staci cheated on you with your twin **brother**. That's low. To beat Staci at her own game (and make no mistake, this is a game – a game that you'll win) you must sink lower and do something more reprehensible. I'd say fucking Staci's mum would fit the bill.
The next time you see your ex, you need to sit her down and explain things, sort of like this:

YOU: Staci, you've ripped my heart out and kicked it around like a football. So I'm going to fuck your mum to even the score, okay?

STACI: Laughter.

Make no mistake, she will laugh at you because she thinks you're speaking out of anger. But you, me and soon Staci and her mother will know just how serious you are.

But, Madame Bitters, I hear you asking, *how do I get Staci's mum to have sex with me?* See how well know you? Here's a three point plan:

1. Go to Staci's mum's house once in a while at first and then more and more often. Be helpful and attentive. Make sure Staci sees all of this going on.

2. Staci will have told her mother by now that you're simply using her to get revenge. Staci's mum won't believe it. She'll likely get angry that her daughter thinks that she can't attract a handsome young man (I'm going to assume you're handsome) without there being an ulterior motive. This will drive a wedge between the two. Use it to your advantage.

3. Continue with step 1, but take it up a notch. Confide to her how much you loved Staci and how badly she hurt you. Every so often pay her a little compliment (a sincere compliment if possible). You could even tell her that you've always had a little crush on her. If that's true, so much the better.

That's pretty much it.

If possible try to get Staci to walk in and catch you and her mum in the act. The next time you see Staci, suggest to her that she might be calling you 'daddy' someday.

Seducing Staci's mother will most likely be a long process. Be patient. The harder you work to get something, the more rewarding it is when it's finally yours.

When Staci finds out what's going on she's going to hate you. That's okay. Deep down beneath the hatred and anger she feels toward you, there will be a grudging respect.

What about brother Keith? I feel confident in stating that he and Staci won't last much longer. Now that you know what's going on, where's the excitement? It's no longer forbidden and therefore not fun anymore. I give them a month – six weeks, tops.

When Staci is no longer part of your lives, you can begin the guilt trip that, if you play your cards right, will last until one of you dies. Nothing's off limits. Ask for money, blood, a kidney, or anything else you can think of. If he balks, gently remind him how he ruined your life by stealing the only girl you ever loved. Try to get other family members to shame him, too. Guilt is the common factor that every family shares. Don't feel guilty for making your brother feel like the piece of shit that he is.
It's just not healthy.

Dear Madame Bitters,

I've got a real dilemma that I hope you can help me with: I'm one of three department heads in a large office. I work closely with another department head "Sue." She wants to be a lot more than just a co-worker, if you know what I mean. In addition to the possibility of being fired, I'm not attracted to this woman at all. Any advice?

Pursued.

Pursued:

Yes, Madame Bitters knows exactly what you mean, you gorgeous hunk of man flesh, and you'd better believe she's got some advice for you. But first, here's a question for you, stud: What's the problem?

Everyone knows that the workplace is a steamy hotbed of sexual intrigue and innuendo. It's the perfect place to find a ready and more than willing partner. If people in the office aren't actually getting it on, you can bet your adorable ass that they're thinking about it.

Your receptionist is thinking about it as she forwards that little encouraging & cutesy email with the kitten hanging on the clothesline to her sister in Romford.

The guy in the cubicle next to yours, who smells like soup, is thinking about it as he Xeroxes personal documents.

And you know how your boss always goes into his office around lunchtime, shuts the door, and sometimes doesn't come out for hours? Well I'm not sure what he's doing in there, but you get my point. While they think and fantasize about it, you actually get to have some - Sex, I mean.

The two of you likely spend at least 40 hours a week together working (hard presumably). Isn't that all the more reason to play together?

So take Madame Bitters advice: Drop a little note to "Sue" instructing her to meet you at your cubicle after-hours. When she does, you bend her over that Xerox machine, hike up her sensible navy skirt, rip those control top pantyhose off her and plow that dimpled ass!
I know you said you weren't attracted to her, but that's the beauty of this particular position – you don't have to look her in the face.

And don't worry about getting fired. If your boss ever brings it up, just tell him that you know exactly what he does in there with the door shut. Even if you don't have any idea what he's doing in there, arch an eyebrow & give him a disapproving look. He'll drop the subject.

Dear Madame Bitters,

Why are you such an uncaring bitch? I've been reading your column ever since you started writing for The Dorking Review, and I am horrified by your "advice." It's not only wrong, but some of your suggestions are dangerous and illegal. Your "advice" is going to hurt someone one day, and then what are you going to do? I don't know how you sleep at night.

Sanctimonious.

Sanctimonious:

You want to know how I sleep at night? Really? All right, I'll tell you.

I sleep in a king-size canopy bed on 500 count Egyptian cotton sheets. I surround myself with pillows that are stuffed only with the finest down.

The mattress I sleep on is made from shredded $100 bills, and the same foam used on NASA space shuttles. This foam works *much* better as a mattress on a bed than as insulation on a space shuttle. Or whatever it is that NASA uses it for.

There now. Do you feel better, Sanctimonious?

Oh, you were asking how I can sleep at night with the knowledge I've ruined or ended so many lives.

For the most part, very well, thank you. I've always had "guilt issues" and by that I mean that I don't feel any. It's just one of the many quirks that makes Madame Bitters what she is.

Now there are some nights when I toss and turn a bit. On these occasions I press a button that's located on my bedside table. It summons Enrique, my 22 year old houseboy. He's always *very* prompt. He's so good at helping me "relax" that afterwards I sleep like a little baby.

A very satisfied little baby.

Madame Bitters

Interviews

An Old Thespian Shares His Thoughts.

Herefordshire is looking particularly beautiful at this time of year. I was visiting my cousin Sherlock, who keeps bees there, near Much Marcle. Yes, in answer to your unspoken question, he was named after his famous great-grandfather on his mother's aunt's side, Sir Leslie Sherlock, the man who introduced barbed wire to Ethiopia. It's purely by coincidence that Sherlock keeps bees in his retirement, as does the fictional detective, Sherlock Holmes. The cocaine habit and violin are two more, less fortunate, coincidences, as I was to discover over the weekend.

Travelling back in the Morgan, I became mired in a hideous traffic jam on the M5. There was a 5 mile tailback. It seems that the Bishop of Gloucester was being transported to a charity 'knock the mitre off the Bishop' event at Teignmouth. Just my luck. These Bishop transporters easily block both carriageways. You'd think they could transport the blighters by air. Though apparently – as I was later informed by Brucie Boulting at the bar of the *Riding Crop and Chastity belt* at Fiddlecombe – there aren't enough spare RAF Hercules at present, and the trains can't cope with that sort of load. (There was something about too many low railway bridges presenting a hazard, given the height of the average Bishop in full regalia complete with mitre, but Brucie and I were on the Calvados by then, so I couldn't swear).

On Monday afternoon, after breakfast, I went back to bed. I finally emerged on Tuesday morning, fit as a fiddle and raring to get back to the memoir I am writing, entitled 'The Memoir I am Writing'. Yes, the title needs work, but then so does the whole thing, as I haven't started it yet. I spent a couple of hours staring out of the study window at old Bellweather, my gardener, wrapping tarred twine around Mrs Thumper, my housekeeper (he tells me it keeps the wasps off her when she's digging, but I don't really care to intrude on the horticultural side of things; damned odd, most of it; still, as long as I get my spuds and cabbages, what do I care; and they do seem to enjoy themselves, those two; reminds me of the time I shared a billet in Glasgow with Gielgud and Richardson, the pantomime horse chaps; they were always tying each other up). And after a couple of hours of that, I gave up and went to the *Non-Sequitur and Mortified Silence* for a stiff one (or three).

Colonel Clasper was there with Alice, his 22 year old 'secretary'. The old goat rambled on and on about the time he found a Chinaman's head under the umbrella stand in Rangoon, all the while staring at Alice's chest and caressing his brandy glass. I was glad to get back home, though I had to rescue Mrs Thumper: Bellweather had tied her to an apple tree and forgotten about her.

I have finally made some progress with the memoir. I am making notes. The plan is, to get as much as I can remember in note form. Raw material, if you like. Then I shall start to order it into something more, er, ordered.

This afternoon, I was thinking of the time when I lived in Paris, after the war. After which war? It doesn't matter, there's always a war somewhere, as Colonel Clasper keeps saying. Determined to become a writer, I did as so many have done before and since. I fled to Paris, and I found a disgusting place to live. I was determined to do two things: To live in poverty, and to produce great literature. Well, I only managed one, and within 3 months I was back in England, playing Wishy Washy in pantomime at Twatton-on-Sea.

Still, I had some experiences that can only be described as experiences. Desperate for money, I took a job at *Madame de Pompadour's* on the Rue des Poissons, playing the piano while the whores went about their whoring. The place was a hideous hole ('a hideous hole filled with hideous holes being filled' was how Lazarre, the barman, described it), but they had a sense of humour. Besides the appalling cheap plonk they dished out, they also served abundant quantities of cake in the *Boudoir d' Antoinette.*

I had to sleep in the attic. There were two hammocks between three of us. My companions were Ligotte, an evil smelling mulatto dwarf covered with tattoos of his favourite goats, and Butto-Butto, a giant, mute pock-marked Lascar who claimed that his left ear had been bitten off by a Marseillaise fishwife.

We had to piss in an 'Emperor' hare-jug, modelled on the Frambois bust of Napoleon.

Every night at 2am, Frou-Frou, the red haired absinthe-drinker, would come up to our attic room, to smoke and talk about her futile passion for Delfine, who specialised in corporal punishment and face sitting.

It was hell in there.

You know, many's the time I've swapped anecdotes with the likes of Brucie or the Colonel and I've thought, 'why aren't I putting this into a story?' Well, the last time I actually said it out loud. 'Why aren't I putting this into a story?' I said. Out loud.

Reminds me of what that bounder Norman Scott thought to himself, when he was rogering that queer liberal, what's his name, Jeremy Thorpe. 'Why aren't I putting this into a Tory?' the blighter thought. A week or two later on, Scott was airing these private speculations with Lord Boothby. When he mentioned the bit about putting it into a Tory, old Boothby said, 'Ah, so you *were* my dear boy, so you *were!'* The most disturbing thing, Scott said afterwards, was the way Boothby was dripping hot candle wax onto a nude photograph of Reggie Kray while he was talking. Scott also reckoned that Boothby had 'Knock before entering' tattooed above his arse.

But it's up to you, whether or not you choose to believe any of this.

It's all pure gossip, old fruit.

Erskin Quint (NS)

THE (ENTERTAINING VETERAN) LIES A MINNELLI INTERVIEW.

"It's nice of you to agree to this interview in the Hob-Nob Hotel here in Brighton, Miss Lies A, even though you have pneumonia."

"What interview? Atishoo! Where are we? Who am I? Atishoo! Please call me Lies A with a zed not a zee."

"Ha, Ha! We love you at Chit-Chat magazine even though you seem to be in a wheelchair again."

"LIFE IS A CABBAGE PATCH OLE CHUM, come on everyone! All together now."

"Please Miss Lies A, don't get up and dance. Damn! Too late."

CRACK! "AAGGHHH! I've broken my hip again."

"You sit back down, and we'll phone the concierge for a sandwich and an ambulance."

"No! Don't bother I've eaten, just pass me that bottle of gin out of my handbag."

"But you've broken one of your hips again."

"I'm used to it. So what was it you wanted? Atishoo!"

"Well Lies A, what was it like being in the same room as Judy?"

"Oh!.. Ok, but Richard was a bit strange. He said that my film 'We're off to see the Wizard' was quite good, then asked if I wanted to play Roxy in 'Chicago'. I said I was far too young to play her, and anyway it went to that Welsh person, Zeta Bryn Teflon or whatever her name is."

"We here at Chit-Chat are a little confused, we didn't know you were in the new Hairy Potter film. We should have done our homework. Anyway, getting back to Judy; we meant Judy, your famous, dead as a doorknob mother, not Judy Flanagan."

"Oh, her. Well she sent me to ballet lessons when I was three, and I broke my hip. She made me have horse riding lessons, and I got pneumonia then broke my hip again. She sent me to gym lessons and I broke both my hips. I even went on the set of her films and got pneumonia again and broke my hips. I went to school with all the other film-star children and broke my hips as well as my knees, and ended up having double pneumonia. Frank Sinatra bounced me on his knee and I broke my hip, had triple pneumonia, had to have both knees replaced and to top it all, a bout of viral encephalitis. I was finally sent to singing lessons and, as they say, the rest is history. LIFE IS A CAMP EX-HUSBAND OLE CHUM! YAAHHH!!!"

"Please stay in your wheelchair Miss Lies A. Shit! Too late."

"AAGGHHH!!! I've broken my ankles, knees, hips, waist, armpits, neck and nose. Atishoo! Ow! It hurts when I sneeze."

"Why do you do this to yourself Lies A?"

"Because the show must go on."

"But you're not getting any younger."

"I know, but; LIFE IS A SPELL IN REHAB OLE CHUM!...Hic..AAGGHHH!!! SHIT! It hurts when I hiccough."

"Please Lies A, get back into your wheelchair. We love you as you are....Well, actually, we love your eyelashes more."

"That's all I'll be remembered for, that and that bloody awful film."

"But Lies A, we all love Cabaret."

"No! Not that film. The other one; New York, New York."

"Oh yes, that one. Still, stop torturing yourself."

"I have to do something better than my mother did, don't I?"

We here at CHIT-CHAT Magazine were lied to. This woman was not who she said she was. We do apologise for any confusion that may have taken place inside your head dear reader. Anyway, Lies A has apparently changed her name to M.J. for some unknown reason.

Previously published in, and subsequently stolen from CHIT-CHAT Magazine. Reprinted here as a warning that some people you meet in life are barefaced liars.

RJH

THE AURORA BOREALIS INTERVIEW

Aurora and I met up in the centre of London for this interview. Aurora wanted to shop for clothes and who could blame her, looking as fabulous as she did. So I agreed.

"Hi there Aurora. Let's go shopping."

"I've already been shopping before you came and bought a new outfit, look!"

She pulled out a really cheap nylon dress from a bag. The label had the name of a fading model that had started to 'design' clothes. Of course, if you can wear clothes then you can surely design them, that's why so many pop stars, celebrities and skinny butt models wake up one morning and say: "Today I'm a fashion designer and if no one buys my cheap outfits, then I'll blame the idiot that actually designed them for me and do something else with my dreary life." This dress was hideous and I didn't want to feel the cheap fabric in case the nylon burnt my fingerprints off.

"Oh look, it's blowing in the wind," I said, while stepping back from the piece of rag.

"Yes, it's like my hair; silky and fine," she said while not noticing me backing into the store.

"Anyway, let's get on with the interview while we look around these clothes. So Aurora, you're very beautiful, why aren't you married? You'd make some man a lovely wife."

"It's true the effects of me being so beautiful must be from the causes I made in the past, but I don't want to make the causes today to become a woman in the future. I'm happy with the way I am."

"That's heavy! Anyway, I thought you'd had the operation, because you've got lovely tits."

"No I'm a cross-dresser, and these are rubber. I've never wanted to be a woman. Look what I can do with these beauties!"

She pushed them right in, and they sprang right back into place. A passing man commented: "Be careful love because you'll damage them doing that. I know, just look at mine." And he opened a large bag and pulled out an enormous damaged pair and swung them in front of us. "I'm taking them back to be mended." He added.

"Oh, I'll have to take more care, won't I?"

"Thank you for that sir," I said, steering Aurora away from him and towards the racks of the latest fashions. "Oh! Look at that blouse. It's very you Aurora."

"You've got a good eye for women's clothes, haven't you Robbie?"

"Tell me about it!"

"Oi! You with the squashed face, I'd like to try this blouse on."

She certainly knew how to treat sales assistants – always be rude to them and they will respect you. She went into the dressing room and shrieked, then rushed out and threw the blouse at the assistant and said: "It's too small. Fetch me another, NOW."
"I'll fetch you one that's four sizes bigger then."

"I'm not that big, bitch."

"Really. That's what all drag queens say."

"Right! That's it, I'll show her," said Aurora in my ear.

"Here you are you fat cow, squeeze yourself and those rubber tits into that if you can."

Aurora was a very cross-dresser at this point and she grabbed the top from the vile assistant and went behind the curtain to try it on. I stood waiting to see what it would look like on her, but it was silent. I looked up at the ceiling and started to whistle to myself, which was strange because I can't whistle. After a while, I noticed smoke coming from behind the curtain. I whispered: "Are you all right in there?"

"Yes of course, I'm having a fag and burning a hole in this blouse, ha, ha, ha! That'll teach her."

I looked around and the assistant was nowhere to be seen. All of a sudden there was a loud scream from behind the curtain and everyone in the store turned to see what was going on. I stuck my head behind the curtain and saw Aurora slapping her breasts and howling. The store manager rushed over with the assistant and I legged it.

I later found out from the hospital that the end of the cigarette had dropped onto her boobs and they'd gone up in flames and melted. A nurse told me there was a bit of scaring, but he'd be OK. Cause and Effect I thought. Cause and Effect.

RJH

THE DORKING REVIEW MEETS SIR BRENT BURTON-TRENCH ON HIS 100TH BIRTHDAY

Today we are honoured to be granted an interview with Dorking's foremost celebrity. Born up the road in Leatherhead, within the Borough of Dorking, Sir Brent Burton-Trench remained, until, aged eleven, he was sent away to boarding school. Alas he was never to return.

Now living on the Isle of Wight – actor, matinee idol, diarist, raconteur – Sir Brent invites Dorking's own Trainee Gossip Correspondent, Timothy Langton, to chat about his famous home and his celebrated life in the arts:-

TIM: Sir Brent. May I start by wishing you a happy birthday. And thanking you on behalf of Dorking for inviting me into your beautiful home.

SIR BRENT: Dear boy! The pleasure is mine.

TIM: You've heard from the Queen?

SIR BRENT: Ha! Yes! Very witty. Dear child.

TIM: You came to the Isle of Wight in the 1940s?

SIR BRENT: That's right. It was 1948. During the run of Coward's

Private Lives at the Vaudeville. I remember us catching the late train to Portsmouth. After the Saturday night show. Then popping on the ferry straight after Sunday morning kippers and brown toast. It was love at first sight.

TIM: You imply "we."

SIR BRENT: Oh; Yes. My assistant. Anthony.

TIM: Ah. Did you know Coward?

SIR BRENT: Know him! We were like brothers. I did all his plays you know. Blithe Spirit. Hay Fever. The Complete Works. Charming man Noel. Supported the Arsenal. I remember him taking me to the 1950 Cup Final. The Gunners. I'm sure that's what he called them. They won 2-0. Do you know what we did to celebrate?

TIM: No.

SIR BRENT: Went backstage to the team bathroom. Then Noel sang to the boys for a complete half an hour. Whilst they splashed about washing the mud off! All his famous songs. Entirely for free. They all loved him. Even footballers. He was like that Noel. Generous to a fault. Beautiful man. Yes.

TIM: Did Mr Coward ever come to the Isle of Wight?

SIR BRENT: Actually no. At least not to stay at Pitchers Bottom. But there's a reason for that. Coward hated the water you know.

TIM: Really?

SIR BRENT: Oh yes. Scared stiff of the sea. Sailed to America in '21 and was as sick as a dog. Hated boats. Once the war ended, flew everywhere did Noel. Like a bird.

PAUSE

We had Novello to stay.

TIM: Ivor Novello?

SIR BRENT: Yes. Cole Porter, Lorenz Hart. They've all been in this room. At that same grand piano.

TIM: Didn't Ivor Novello write "We'll Gather Lilacs"?

SIR BRENT: Well yes. I believe he did.

TIM: My favourite song. "We'll walk together down an English lane – Until our hearts have learned to sing again – When you come home once more."

Are you alright sir?

SIR BRENT: Fine! Don't mind me.

TIM: Have I said anything to upset you?

SIR BRENT: No dear boy. No. Sorry.

TIM: What was he like?

SIR BRENT: Who?

TIM: Ivor Novello.

SIR BRENT: Oh. Him.

TIM: Great song writer. Genius. Didn't he also write "Keep The Home Fires Burning?

SIR BRENT: Yes, I believe he did.............Look.................If you must know, Novello was a bastard.

TIM: I've upset you haven't I?

SIR BRENT: No.

TIM: It was you who brought him up.

SIR BRENT: Quite. I really am most terribly sorry. The song; We'll gather lilacs. That English lane. It's right there. Outside the back door. Takes you down to Swanley's Folly. Pretty little lane. We'll gather lilacs. Yes. That was the last I saw of Anthony.

TIM: Sorry?

SIR BRENT: Novello. Stole my assistant. Just like that. Left high and dry. After thirteen bloody years. Had to start signing my own photographs. Darn my own socks. Make the bed.

TIM: You never married?

SIR BRENT: Yes. What? Marriage? No. Thought about it of course. One always thinks about these things. Never seemed to come across the right girl. Never at the right moment. Ships passing in the night I suppose.

TIM: So you moved to the Isle of Wight.

SIR BRENT: Yes. Summer of 49. Seven thousand pounds this house cost me. Do you know what it's worth now?

TIM: Gosh, I don't know. A fortune.

SIR BRENT: Go on. Take a guess.

TIM: A million pounds.

SIR BRENT: Treble it.

TIM: Three million!

SIR BRENT: And the rest.

TIM: Wow! Must be the finest house on the Island.

SIR BRENT: We did things to it, naturally. Bathrooms, the pool, that rose garden. Yes. Novello died suddenly you know. '51 that would have been. Bastard. Coronary thrombosis.

TIM: So your Assistant came back?

SIR BRENT: You mean Anthony? No. Anthony went to America. Drifted around I'm told. Usual stuff. Started working for Rock Hudson apparently.

TIM: You keep in touch?

SIR BRENT: Mmm? Oh no. He died. I think. Yes.That would have been the 80's. Lots died around that time. Back in those days.

TIM: You played Romeo on seven occasions.

SIR BRENT: That's right. The first one was 1932. For the opening of the new theatre in Stratford. With Hermione Langrage as Juliet. And dearest Vernon Peacock as my Mercutio. Yes. The last was at the Theatre Royal Windsor. Shortly after my sixtieth birthday. I remember the Duke of Edinburgh coming back after I'd taken seventeen curtain calls. With Benjamin Britten as I remember.

TIM: You knew Britten.

SIR BRENT: But of course. Everyone did. Although it was Peter who was my closest friend.

TIM: The tenor Peter Pears?

SIR BRENT: Yes. They had the Red House in Aldeburgh, and I had the Pink House in Pitchers Bottom. They came to stay for a fortnight every summer. Then I'd go back to theirs. Benjamin used to tease Peter that he and I were two shades of the same colour.

TIM: Some critics used to compare you to Sir John Gielgud.

SIR BRENT: Gosh, you have been doing your homework. Yes. That's true enough. Johnny and me were always going up for the same things.

PAUSE

What I mean is, we often went up for the same part. In a play. Or film.

TIM: Did you ever share the same stage?

SIR BRENT: Oh no. That would have been quite wrong. We both knew. We were far too similar you see. If one was giving his Hamlet, the other would do his Henry. Of course we would always meet up afterwards. Lamb chops in the Savoy. Sparkling wine with spotted dick. The whole gang. Swap notes. Sign autographs. That sort of stuff.

TIM: Gielgud stayed here didn't he. At the Pink House?

SIR BRENT: How do you know that?

TIM: It's in Sir John's autobiography. Page 438;

SIR BRENT: Ah; You are referring to my Silver Jubilee Weekend Party in 1977. Yes, Johnny came. Along with half of London. As I recall he arrived on the Friday and left before breakfast on the Saturday. Tuppy Brimstone said something about Binkie Beaumont. Can't tell you what. Even now. Anyway, Johnny told Toad to organise an immediate departure. So yes. Johnnie did stay. But only for one night.

TIM: Do you mind if I ask. Who was Toad? There's no reference to him in the Gielgud book.

SIR BRENT: Neither should there be. Toad was Johnny's Personal Assistant. He had nothing whatsoever to do with his public life. Any gentleman must surely be allowed to draw the line somewhere. Draw the distinction. Yes.

TIM: I see.

SIR BRENT: Yes. There's public and there's private. Ne'er the twain should meet. He was a splendid chap Toad. Loyal to a fault. Did everything for Johnny. Right to the end.

TIM: Of course. You love this Island, don't you sir.

SIR BRENT: The Isle of Wight. Oh yes. It's been more than a home. Or a haven. I suppose you could say it's been my mother. In a strange sort of way. Maybe my wife even. My sanctuary. It's...

PAUSE

People here are quiet. We keep ourselves to ourselves. The little things are far more important than the so-called big things. The stuff newspapers are interested in. The Tittle-tattle.

TIM: So you'll be staying here.

SIR BRENT: I shall die here. Hopefully in this chair. Chatting to someone pleasant such as yourself. Drinking a pink gin. If I'm lucky.

TIM: There's a reception this evening.

SIR BRENT: Yes.

TIM: And a dinner.

SIR BRENT: I know. The Lord Mayor has been very kind.

TIM: You must be excited.

SIR BRENT: Excited! Ah yes. I remember. No dear boy. Excited isn't the word. Content. You do realise I don't know anybody any more. They've all gone.

TIM: You're getting the Freedom Of The Island.

That makes you friends with everyone.

SIR BRENT: How terrifying.

TIM: Mmmmm. You're not afraid of anybody are you?

SIR BRENT: No. Not any more.

TIM: Did you ever get stage fright?

SIR BRENT: Oh yes. Once upon a time. I was always scared of what people might think.

TIM: But now you're not.

SIR BRENT: No. There's no point any more. Time's moved on. Those days are long gone.............. You're coming tonight?

TIM: Me? You must be joking. They only give two tickets to the press. One for the Editor, and one for his wife.

SIR BRENT: I said you are coming. I want you to come. I want someone I can talk to. I want you to be sitting there. Beside me.

TIM: But...

SIR BRENT: No buts. It's been decided. Now be off with you, before I change my mind.

PAUSE

Can you drive?

TIM: Well yes as a matter of fact.

SIR BRENT: Good. We'll take the Roller. I take it you can drive a Rolls Royce Phantom? Good. Come back at seven.

TIM: But...

SIR BRENT: You've a date with a girl?

TIM: Oh no. I haven't a girlfriend.

SIR BRENT: Good. That's settled then. Be here for seven. And bring your toothbrush.

Juanita Juan

AN EVENING WITH MISS DORIS DOO DAH, DOO DAH

We were invited to spend an evening in the theatre with Miss Doris Doo Dah, Doo Dah. It was one of those evenings where she would sing a few songs and then the audience would ask her a few light-hearted questions. Unfortunately, Miss Doo Dah, Doo Dah didn't have a vast repertoire, in fact she only had one and a half songs, because her musical director dropped down dead while composing her second song: "Acne Is For Teenage Girls (that's why you adore older women like me)." She would hum the last part.

I'd like to say I enjoyed the evening....BUT, when someone insists that they look like Cheryl Cole all night, one feels like ripping their arms off just to spite their sleeves, but Doris didn't have any arms, which spoilt the crescendo parts of the one whole song she sung, because she couldn't thrust them in the air for dramatic effect, like those tune-less divas we all know and hate.

So there we were. All the unfortunates Brighton had to offer piling into the bar after a very short first half, which consisted of Doris playing some castanets (between her knees). A wino who had won ten tickets plus drinks to the show from a radio phone-in – apparently he was asked by the station's DJ what the words were to the second part of Doris's unfinished song, he hadn't got a clue but started to hum, and without realizing it won the competition – had asked for his prize of champagne for ten of his wino friends to be delivered to them on the banquette in the corner of the elegant rococo theatre bar. The barman gave them Meths in a silver ice bucket and they lapped it up oblivious to what it tasted like.

When the bell went for the second part of the show, these two very drunken drag queens started to fight and were quickly thrown out of the theatre. I found out later they'd both been heavyweight boxers in the past and they had thought that the boxing ring bell had gone off.

We settled into our seats and the curtain went up, and there was Doris standing in a single spotlight in the same evening dress as the first half. She started to sing and someone in the front row screamed so loud, Doris nearly jumped out of her dress and promptly stopped.

I found out later that this woman planned it so Doris would stop singing, and it worked. Doris composed herself after her heart rate slowed back down and said:

"So, Ladies and Gentlemen, I think we'd better have the first question. Yes! You with the tattooed forehead."

"Is that the only bloody frock you've got Doris"?

"No! I have lots of these at home. Because I look like Cheryl Cole I had to come on the bus in disguise, and I could only manage to bring my purse, a frock and a wig with me."

"You don't look like Cheryl Cole you silly bitch," shouted someone in a batwing peach coloured cardigan (I think it was a man).

"I'll have you know people are always telling me I look like her."

"More like Old King Cole, ha, ha, hic," slurred a wino that was lying on the floor with a copy of a 1987 Vogue magazine – the one with the 'black is the new pink' feature in it.

"Oh is that Cheryl's father"?

The audience looked bewildered, the voice said: "Of course you couldn't carry lots of things because you haven't got any arms you silly cow. In fact you can't even carry a tune." This from a man who was fast asleep, and was then nudged awake by his wife so he could hear Doris's answer to his profound insightful observations.

"I don't know how you could say such horrible things. You were snoring all the way through my castanet act."

"Why Doo Dah, Doo Dah"? Said a very sad looking woman in the stalls. I found out later that she had had her face lowered instead of lifted because she'd been put on the operating table upside down and the surgeon hadn't noticed so he pulled it all upwards, but when she sat round the right way it was all stretched downwards.

"Perhaps he doesn't like my singing voice."

"No. Why is your name Doo Dah, Doo Dah"?

"Because I come from Kemp Town, and the Kemp Town ladies sing this song."

"DOO DAH, DOO DAH," sang everyone in the audience. There was clapping and screaming. It was the best part of a very confusing night.

"It's Camptown, not Kemp Town," said a wino.

"But have you ever been to Keep Town"?

"No"!

"I thought not, otherwise you'd understand."

All the queens in the audience burst into laughter and gave a knowing nod, some even whinnied and shouted "Giddy up Girlfriend," one man cantered to the loo and back in what looked like a new pair of gold glitter slingbacks.

"We'd better move on or this concert is gwine to run all night, gwine to run all day. Perhaps it's time I sang another song."

"AAAGGGHHHHH!! NO," screamed everyone. And then a large booming voice from the seats up in the Gods said: "You obviously know the Stephen Collins Foster (1826-1864) Camptown races song"?

"I certainly doo-dah, doo-dah"

Everyone laughed.

"Anyway, you haven't told us why you were picked to play the part of a woman who gets bitten by a mosquito, then gets malaria and has to go and have extensions put in her hair and is then convinced she's a singer, in your new film."

"Oh! You mean 'Hair Sick' I was chosen because I sound like Cheryl Cole. It was only one day's work in the studio doing the voice over, but we had so much fun that day, me and the other person who's in the film.

"So, it's a cartoon"? Said a disappointed looking woman... Why I don't know.

"Yes, but I'll be doing more films in the future. Perhaps I'll audition for the part of Cheryl Cole when they make a film about her very interesting life. Let's hope they will."

"What about Nat King Cole"? Yawned one of the winos whose friends had all fallen asleep;

"Someone mentioned him before. I'm not sure I could play her father in a film as well. I would have to do some research on him. Sounds quite interesting though, and would stretch me as an actress."

"It certainly would, because he was black and you're not," said an elderly man in the front row.

"I think I could do black, apparently it's very hard to do, much harder than a serious role, but I'm definitely up for a challenge."

The audience looked bewildered again, then to make matters worse, someone shouted: "What about Natalie"?

"Ah! I presume you mean Cheryl's mother. I didn't know her name was Natalie. I would love to play her as well; in fact I could play every part, now that would be really challenging."

"It certainly would, he's dead and she's just had a new liver given to her," shouted some woman in the Royal Box.

"That's OK because I'm a method actress who can pretend to be dead. Look."

She held her breath and didn't flinch once. In fact a lot of people went for a drink at the bar and phoned their babysitters to see if their children were all right. Doris was still holding her breath when everyone returned to their seats. She exhaled and said: "See. I looked quite dead didn't I"?

We all nodded, but couldn't have cared less.

"But you didn't look as black as my gin-soaked liver," said the woman in the Royal Box.

"Oh! You again. But I can cook liver and bacon just like a mother would for her daughter and dead father."

A stagehand entered with a gas hob and a frying pan and Doris started to cook some liver and bacon. It must have been planned because why would they conveniently have a hob and some liver and bacon backstage. Perhaps her management team thought there might be a lull in people asking questions, so they planted a woman in the Royal Box to ask Doris certain questions relating to liver and bacon to fill the gaps. The smell of cooking woke the winos up, and they moved towards the front of the stage with their hands held out. Doris tried to lift the pan with her feet but it went flying into the air and all over the winos who had to be removed to hospital suffering from third degree burns.

Doris managed to pull herself onto a stool and said: "That's the trouble with having no arms, it's a bugger trying to serve food to people, whether it be a bijou dinner party at home or a charity event feeding of thousands of starving people in a third world country;" "What happened to them"?

"They probably died of starvation."

"No, your arms," said the woman.

"They were misplaced years ago. In fact that's when people started to tell me I looked like Cheryl Cole, when I lost my arms."

"I'll bet my money on a bob-tail nag that people were just saying that to avoid talking about the pain you were going through, and you probably became a singer and actress because it went to your head hearing all that un-real adulation."

There was a long silence, and then Doris started to cry. Someone next to me coughed because their stomach had just jumped up into their throat. I passed a hanky, and she burst out sobbing too. It was the worst night I have ever experienced in my life.

Doris finally pulled herself together and said in a trembling voice: "I think you're right. I've never thought of it before because my ego has got in the way, so I think I'll sing you all a song before I retire from show business for ever."

"AAAGGGHHH!!!!! DORIS NOOOO" we all screamed as we bolted out of the theatre leaving Doris standing there feeling devastated and all alone.

Doris has since entered the 'You've Got No Talent Get Over It' competition. Should you meet her, please let her know that the

Failed Actors & Singers Guild have a £7.50 royalty cheque for her, for the awful film she did in 2010.

RJH

MAJOR TOM & MISS VERA

Tom Tellitasitis, a retired Major, was in for a bit of a surprise when I, Purl Pratt, went to interview him for the *Let's Get It On,* Internet dating agency Magazine. It was a Friday afternoon when I entered the gold wallpapered lounge of 'THE' most desirable man on the planet. It was one of those moments when you think to yourself; eat your heart out George Clooney.

I'd started the internet dating agency two years previously, and had no idea there were so many desperately lonely old people out there who wanted some sort of partner. There were people who were so desperate that if I'd sent them on a date with a spoon they'd have felt sufficiently stirred. (Ha, ha, ha! I used to be a comedienne).

The Major had joined the agency just after his wife, Tabitha had died. Apparently, she'd been to a bull fight in Spain and the bull had spotted her in the crowd in her bright crimson camisole top and matching puffball skirt and charged at her. After she'd run round and round the stadium for hours the bull finally caught up with her and thrust his horns right up the back of her puffball. She went flying through the air to the sounds of "Vamos and Allay." Fortunately, her puffball skirt acted like a parachute and Tabitha landed on the hard arena ground safely. Unfortunately, she was already dead from the bull's gouging of her pear-shaped buttocks – Did you know that a survey on a group of women with apple and pear shaped bums found that pear-shaped bums had their memory impaired and apple shaped ones didn't, and here's the actual proof. Tabitha must have had impaired memory that day when she put the crimson outfit on to wear to the bull fight because, ER, HELLO! Nine bulls out of ten prefer the colour crimson.

Anyway, after the funeral there was no mourning for the Major. He went straight onto our dating site and filled in all his details. We only had a Miss Vera on the books who matched his requirements. The Major was reluctant to converse at first because of his shyness, but after Vera had offered him as much sex as he wanted, whenever and wherever, he gave in and exchanged phone calls as well as e-mails with her. Then apparently it all went pear-shaped – just like his missus' bum.
I wanted to find out what really happened.

"So, Major Tom, we would like to hear what really went on between you and Vera so we can warn others. It's always a risk in these perilous internet dating games we all partake in when we're sad, lonely and desperate.

"I blamed you at first Purl, but then I realized you were extremely good at your job. She was everything I asked for and more."

"We do our best. So when did it all start?"

"When she sent me this oil painting to hang on the wall. It got my juices flowing so I decided I would meet her."

"I suppose just for a drink to start with?"

"No. Full on sex. I mean just look at her!"

"I thought you were shy Major Tom?"

"Only about being nude. I'd never even shown my wife of thirty years what I looked like in the buff. We were taught in the Army to always keep our clothes on in case the enemy burst in and caught us with our trousers down."

"I see."

"Sadly we didn't get that far because she said she'd just come back from visiting her daughter in jail in Sakar, Turkey. Those damn Turks had kidnapped her and wanted £500,000. Miss Vera was very distraught. She played me the ransom tape and all I could hear were the screams of her daughter being tortured. Those blasted Turks were still at war with the English I thought."

"She wasn't your daughter, so why help her?"

"Because her daughter was in the Women's Air Corps. I couldn't let her down, could I?" But in all the commotion I should have known something was up because she said her daughter was doing her eleven plus when we first spoke but I'd forgotten. She made me feel responsible for her daughter."

"Turkey's not at war with England is it?"

"Not now, no! I was confused what with all the sex that was on offer to me. I thought I was falling in love with Vera, especially when I kissed her scrumptious thighs before going to bed every night – on the picture of course."

"Sex and love always get mixed up, they are not the same thing. We try to stress that on our dating site but people never seem to learn."

"I know now Purl, but what else could I do? I put the money into her account. She then said, 'I can't wait for us to be alone together so I can grind your loins and wear you out with passion'. We were all set on meeting, when she suddenly phoned and said her business had been taken off her by the taxman. She owed one million pounds in back taxes. She then played me a tape of herself being tortured by the taxman. She screamed; "Please no! Don't stretch my luscious body on this awful rack." and "Please, no more water boarding, I haven't got my tiny bikini on." I couldn't bear hearing her scream any longer so I paid the money into her account."

"What was this 'so called' business called?"

"Can Tank R Us. She supplied tanks to the British Army. I couldn't let my country down could I? Besides she knitted me this sleeveless tank top as a thank you."

"She saw you coming. One million, five hundred thousand pounds for a picture and a knitted tank top. She never mentioned being a psychic I suppose?"

"Was she?"

"Of course. Look, it's sleeveless."

"Oh! Yes it is Purl."

"Anyway, do carry on Major Tom."

"Well she certainly played on my insecurities as well as my organisational skills, which I learnt while in the Army. She was so grateful to me that we had phone sex. She said rub my buttocks and lick my nipples. I mean what could I do? I was madly in love with her, then just before I nearly had an orgasm she told me that her poor mother had fallen from the top of the Eiffel Tower and broke both her legs and wrist."

"ONLY HER LEGS AND WRIST!"

"I should have guessed, but I was in the throes of having an orgasm. Her mother was modelling clothes up the Eiffel Tower for Chanel when a gust of wind blew up the silk chiffon poncho she was wearing and over the edge she went. The poncho was for the spring collection, and waiting on the ground below were all the other famous Parisian designers who saw the design and copied it. She had to pay Chanel four million pounds for loss of income, as well as the hospital, and Swiss clinic bills – where she had to recuperate. What with Vera, her daughter and now her mother all suffering, I felt like part of the family, so I paid the four million, five hundred thousand pounds into Vera's bank account."

"WHAT!"

"Yes I know Purl. She said she was on her way around here for lots of sex after having her hair shaved from her armpits and her crutch, but that was six months ago. I've been well and truly F****D haven't I?"

"Well I have some news for you. I've recently found out that Vera was a MAN!"

"WHAT! A MAN! Well at least we didn't have, you know, real sex. The thought of two sweating male bodies writhing around naked on a bed doesn't bear thinking about does it?"

"But in your head you rubbed his buttocks, licked his nipples and kissed his scrumptious thighs, didn't you Major Tom?"

I suddenly froze with a lump in my throat as he turned to me with a lump in his trousers.

"Mmm! I did didn't I. Do you knit Purl?"

"AAGHH! KNIT ONE PURL'S GONE. BYE!"

RJH

AN INTERVIEW WITH COUNT DRACULA (RETIRED)

I arrived at the Count's home and was invited in by his long time secretary, Olga Von Tin. She directed me to a small but pleasant study where I was seated in front of a huge desk. Half an hour later, the Count entered the room. I stood and introduced myself, the Count ignored me and sat behind his desk, poured a drink and spoke.

"Ask der questions."

"Why did you retire Sir?"

"Enough vid der sir! Call me Drac! I kept flying into zer trees, mein eyesight is kaput! I voz loosink more blood den I could drink, an zo......I haff to stop."

"That must have been a hard decision to make after so many years of vamping."

"Is dis boyshik narish?! How much blood should I lose!"

"You decided to sell up and move to Florida, why?"

"It's vot ve do, it's der oranges."

"Have you still got the castle in Transylvania?"

"I've rented it to dis fella called Frankenstein. Oye vot a shunda! I certainly created a monster for mine self there, the guy is meschuge! You know; crazy, he vonts to turn it into ein theme park for der tourists."

"Will you let him do that?"

"If der sheckles are right."

"What do you do with your time now?"

"Vel, I haff expanded mein plasma collection, started zer sonar station for der bats, other den dat, I hang around der house till zer sunset."

"Do you ever worry that a vampire hunter will find you and try to exterminate you?"

"I'm over a thousand years old, vot do you think Shirley!"

"Where do you get your blood from these days?"

"Journalists.".......

GH

TRAVEL

GLOUCESTER –
STRANGERS IN A STRANGE LAND

Peregrine Trip investigates the West Country cathedral city...

I stared intently at the map, but I was just not seeing. For the life of me, I could not locate Bristol Road.

So, feeling rather foolish, I asked the thick-set lad at reception who was trying to give me directions: "I'm sorry, but which is Bristol Road? I know...I'm sorry...it's stupid but I just can't see it."

The pair of receptionists began laughing. "My God, they must think I'm a complete plank," I thought to myself.

"On no, mate. It ain't really Brizzle Road, it's Maniac Street*... there, see? Oi jes' calls it the Brizzle Road!"

Directions from the city centre multi-storey to a car park more convenient for the hotel at once became crystal clear.

Thus *was Gloucester strangeness 1.*

Mrs and I had decided to drive down on the Saturday, look at the Cathedral and the local architecture, including the rejuvenated docks, spend the night and return on Sunday.

Parking in the centre, we located Tourist Information and asked them to help us find a room. They placed us in one of those standard city centre jobs – a little tired and in need of some refurbishment, but comfortable.

We found it easily enough on foot and encountered our friends at reception. One, taller, seemed to take responsibility for all the official bits and pieces and it was only when we asked about parking nearer did his mate start chipping in with the Bristol Road nonsense.

"Oi jes' calls it the Brizzle Road!" I determined to shove a bar stool up his Bristol Road before we left.

I will pass on singing the praises of Gloucester Cathedral – others far more knowledgeable than I have written with greater eloquence about this splendid church than I ever could. We visited and, awed, moved on.

Having determined we would eat at a Southern American-style restaurant, Old Orleans, in the old docks area, we cleaned up in our room and headed down to the bar for a refresher before walking to dinner.

Gloucester strangeness 2: There, in the hotel lounge bar, sitting on her own at a window seat, was a bride. We knew she was a bride because she was wearing the traditional garb. We smiled at her, got our drinks and sat down at our own table.

Another, more outgoing couple entered. On seeing the young woman, they started up: "Ooh, just married eh?"

"at's roight."

"Where's the groom then?"

"Oi dunno," she smiled, a little bewildered. "e jes' went off with the best man and the ushers and everyone. Oi didn't know Oi were gettin' married 'til this mornin'. He planned everything... got me parents in on it and even bought me dress. Now Oi dunno wha's 'app'nin'."

Bless her, she didn't seem at all put out at being abandoned in a hotel bar. She just kept smiling and laughing as a bunch of strangers decided that they would not leave a bride on her own.

Anyway, we had a table booked at Old Orleans. It was pleasant enough, if quiet, and the food was more than passable.

Earlier in the day we had spotted a traditional old-fashioned looking pub hard by the Cathedral precinct. We decided to pop in on our way back to the hotel and hopefully try some local brew.

Gloucester strangeness 3: as we walked through the door, I swear conversations stopped and people turned to look.

This was a city centre pub!

We ordered some local brew, but I'm afraid to say we lost interest as we felt extremely uncomfortable and decided to end our evening in the hotel bar. At least we might ascertain what happened to the lonely bride.

Back at the hotel, we nosed into the lounge where we had encountered her — she wasn't there. Behind the bar was the taller of our two receptionist friends and I asked him for our drinks.

Gloucester strangeness 4: "Oi'm sorry, Oi'm closing... there's no-one in."

"Er, we're guests and *we're* in. Surely we're entitled to bar service?"

"Oh, 's'all roight, yew can still get a drink in t'other bar across the 'all there. That'll be open for ages yet."

Relieved, we headed across the hall, pushed open the doors, headed toward the bar and found ourselves in the middle of... a bloody wedding party! The lone bride's wedding party. The bar was at the other end of this long reception room and for the second time this evening all eyes were on us as we made our way towards a drink. Needless to say, we didn't stay – we took our nightcaps to our room and drank them perched on the end of the bed, watching *Match of the Day*. Neither of us could summon the nerve to go back for another, so we retired somewhat early.

The following morning was grey and drizzly. The weather failed to make the rejuvenated docks with their antique centres, craft shops and coffee bars look very interesting and we were, to be honest, rather fed up with the place. We headed home.

On Monday, hearing that we'd spent the weekend there, a colleague said to Mrs: "What on earth dragged you there? I could have told you – Gloucester's bloody odd!"

I have no conclusive evidence that would allow me to tell you with any certainty what happened to the colleague. But Mrs never mentions her these days, nor have I seen the blouse and skirt she wore to work that Monday after the Gloucester sojourn.

(*Unfortunately, I can't remember the road's actual name. PT*)

SM

ANTWERP, ART AND ALE –
A TRAVELLER'S DIARY.

Travel editor Peregrin Trip visits the historic Belgian port...

Magnificent! Antwerp Central railway station – truly magnificent.

What a temple to the glory days of rail travel! *Antwerpen Centraal* was clearly designed to demonstrate that the latter-day burghers' ambition and civic pride were just as great as their medieval forefathers who built its more ancient and holier compatriot down the road, the Cathedral. The architecture itself is gasp-worthy enough – but then you notice the practicality of the design: the station is not a broad, 20-track-wide estuary of railway lines it is deep, the tracks and platforms built above and beneath each other. Marvellous use of space.

The woman in tourist information insists there's no need to take a taxi to our hotel as she draws our route to it on a map.

Two false turns, one dinged holdall-heaving shoulder and a sweat-soaked back later, we find home for the next three nights. I shall not dwell on the Ibis Centrum – suffice to say, don't over pack. The designer has never heard of wardrobe or drawer space.

Bearings established, we head for the *Grote Markt* and there, in the corner, is one of the reasons we're here – a bar with 'De Koninck' emblazoned above its windows. *Den Engel* is a typical *bruin kroeg*, ideal for sucking up the atmosphere and sampling the local brew. "Why are people talking about 'bollocks' when they talk about the local beer?" We ponder. "There was a bar on the way here called *'t Bolleke* - can that have anything to do with it?"

Dinner – *De Valk*. Mrs has the croquettes followed by Flanders stew, I try the tomato soup and the unpronounceable but edible chicory wrapped in ham in a cheese sauce. This is Belgium, so of course it is good – but we agree we've had better, and we will again.

As Friday promised to be overcast, we decide this is the day for the Fine Arts Museum (Saturday's forecast is for sun, so clearly the day for exploration). So we stroll the 15-20 minutes to the grand *Koninklijk Museum voor Schone Kunsten* (art galleries in German and Dutch-speaking lands always prompt schoolboy giggles: "*Kunst* - tee hee!"). Once in the entrance hall, Mrs strolls confidently up to the man at the desk and asks for two tickets.

"I em shawry, but de musheum is closhed for refurbishment," he apologises. My shoulders drop. Can this be? We joke with friends that everywhere we go, there's some major attraction that we can't see because of scaffolding – but a whole, major gallery closed at once? Not bit by bit? "OK – so we missed the Van Dykes – good reason to come back. I did like those Rubens, though."

I have never been more impressed by a head-butt than the one I saw Mrs deliver onto the nose of the bearer of the bad news that we wouldn't be viewing the collection today. It was accompanied by a satisfying or sickening – depending on your point-of-view, I imagine – crunching sound as the cartilage suffered the trauma of the impact. However, I had little time to admire her "headiwork" as it were, as the man's colleague made a move towards the desk. I intervened, my knee found his soft 'centre of gravity' and he doubled over and hit the floor. My effort was particularly gratifying, not least because of its speed – I had been suffering with painful and swollen knees and ankles thanks to the cold weather recently, but they clearly did not hinder my ability to act. The chap behind the counter, all bloody nose, looking bemused, made a grab for the telephone. But he'd clearly had enough so I stepped in, took Mrs by the elbow and guided her to the door.

"We can always come back at another time. What shall we do with the morning instead?"

"This is Belgium – there's bound to be something half-decent in the Cathedral. In fact I believe there's a Rubens in there."

Well, what a piece of luck! There is a special exhibition of triptychs, altar pieces and what-have-you from the museum we've just failed to enjoy, in the Cathedral. We spend a very satisfactory 90 minutes or so enjoying these gifts commissioned by the old guilds, ears glued to the entertaining dramatized commentaries.

Lunch provides the solution to the *bolleke* conundrum. I ask the waiter about the difference between the two versions of De Koninck on offer at this *Grote Markt* bar/restaurant – the *bolleke* and the *prinz*. Well, it's simply that the *bolleke* is the chalice-shaped glass designed to deliver an inch-thick head with your 25cl of beer. The *prinz* is a simple slim, straight glass.

Aha!

"This afternoon, why don't we have a look at the Maritime Museum? It's just round the corner from here," Mrs hints.

"Why not? This place must have a rich maritime history – wealthy and important port, rival to the Hanseatic ports and all that."

The Maritime Museum is indeed round the corner from the *Grote Markte* and housed in a delightful Gothic fortress.

At the entrance, my attention is attracted by a sign on a huge antique wooden door – rather thoughtfully, it is in English as well as Flemish: "The Museum is closing..." some other information about events in a park later this summer, but I was too disappointed to take in the information.

There was a sharp cracking sound behind me. I turned just in time to see Mrs deliver a karate kick at a fence post which, under this second assault, gave way. I am compelled to remark on the splendidly athletic manner in which she grabbed the post and hurled it, javelin-like, through the window of the ticket office. Most Olympian. I gathered, as the place was closed, there was no-one on the other side of the glass – there was certainly no discernible blood spatter on the window's remnants. But not wishing to see the job left half done, I hefted one of the medieval cannonballs from a nearby display and put it through the remaining glazing. For completeness's sake, she grabbed her javelin from the office interior and took care of the window frames – they rather looked as if they could use some renovation themselves.

The rest of the old town's river front is disappointingly unprepossessing, with just a steel-and-glass bar/café to attract the attention. We didn't investigate the docks or the rest of the river since boat trips don't begin until later in the year.

Now, today, Friday, was her birthday and Mrs fancied dinner at the recommended Brasserie Appelmans. It was a good choice... although we had to wait for a table, the Manhattans at the bar were first-class and the delay was only about 20 minutes, after which the inexplicably apologetic waiter led us to a splendid window table on the first floor.

Eschewing a starter in favour of an anticipated dessert, she plumped for the lamb fillet. "The best lamb I have ever had in my life," she declared. My pork was tender and tasty but I'm afraid the best I ever had was a couple of hundred miles away in Paris.

To the Rubens House on Saturday morning. An excellent and informative 90-minute introduction to the life of the Flemish master and a magnificent house giving the lie to the idea that all artists struggled to survive in cold, dank garrets. The changing status of the artist in 17th century Flanders encapsulated in one enthralling display.

The *Meir* is a splendid shopping drag and after our Rubensian sojourn, we joined its throng – the good people of Antwerp and its environs joined by tourists in the Saturday sunshine. I had spotted some boots the previous evening and thought to buy a pair. "You need a 42 in European sizes," Mrs said.

The assistant returned from the stock room with, of course a 41 and a 43. "You could try them just in case..."

Have you ever hauled a fitted shelf system from a shop wall? It is most gratifying. I can recommend steel ones particularly as a loosened steel bar is ideal for demolishing other fittings. I was however, denied much further expression of my ire, as Mrs had lifted a loose shoe stand above her head and heaved it at the assistant who had suggested I try on ill-fitting shoes: "You can seriously damage people's feet like that," she advised.

I had more luck next door, where she spotted a delightful pair of fawn brogue ankle boots. They fit like a glove and I wore them that very evening.

But I get ahead of myself. After lunch at the Rubens House Inn we head for the *Museum Mayer van den Bergh* which is a delightful little gallery (if over-warm – they were probably caught out by the sudden nice weather). The highlights are a couple of pieces by Pieter Bruegel the Elder, especially the *Dulle Grite,* or *Angry Maggie* – a startling and engrossing piece of Renaissance unfathomability. Brilliant.

After the museum, it's such a lovely afternoon we decide to sit for a while at a café in front of the Cathedral. My ankle is beginning to complain anyway so it's a good plan. As are the *bollekes* we down in the sunshine. Conversation is rendered virtually impossible for a good half hour, though, by bell practice or something. They are loud bells.

Our final Flemish dinner finds us in the *Grote Markte* again where she decides to essay the mussels – sorry, *mosselen* – at last. I go for the mixed grill. Both are as they should be – it is a bar/restaurant, not an *à la carte* place – and we are satisfied.

We check out of the Ibis Centrum at 12 noon on Sunday. I hand in the key, expecting that to be that. But: "Did you hef breakfasht deesh mawning?" The young lady at reception asks. "Yes." "Vell dat ish twenty-four Eurosh, I'm afraid. Did you hef breakfast every day?" Despite our protestations that we had paid for B&B in advance the staff insisted that we couldn't have and I was obliged to cough up 72 Euros. I was not impressed since, as I indicated, neither was I pleased with the size of the room. But upon ascertaining they would not charge me for the service, I asked them to call a taxi to take us to the station (we weren't risking the walk again)...

The smashing noise was the large glass fruit bowl from a reception table – Mrs had hurled it at the lift doors. Her follow-through brought her into a convenient distance from a gift display cabinet which she upended with ease, scattering playing cards, key rings, lighters and all manner of cheap souvenirs across the lobby. Meanwhile, I had separated the telephones from the reception counter and ripped out all the wiring. The counter itself was surprisingly loosely connected to the floor and was constructed from a very flimsy ply which splintered into fragments all too easily. The assorted bottles behind the adjacent bar exploded in rainbow sprays of colour when hit by flying bar stools – a late and fitting contribution to the city's illustrious art history.

A final view of the magnificent railway station frontage as we pull up in the taxi is our last memory of a wonderful visit to a most attractive city. We must return – the Fine Arts Museum owes us.

SM

TRAVEL GUIDE: LIVERPOOL

There can be fewer more beautiful cities than the jewel on the Mersey that is Liverpool.

Once home to the Beatles, this lively metropolitan city sees visitors come from all over the world to visit Penny Lane, Strawberry Fields, and search in vain for Abbey Road (which is in London). The Cavern is a Mecca for these ardent, travel-weary Beatles fans, although the original club has long since become a travel-agent.

But Liverpool has more to offer the seasoned traveller than mere Beatles tat sold by raven haired Scousers. There are the twin cathedrals, the twin football grounds and the "Twins" on Lime Street (very reasonable, pleasure guaranteed). The architecture of the city lends this iconic land a distinctive look without rival. Many of the buildings come from an era when Liverpool was the world hub of the slave trade, but this is quietly forgotten amid debates of exactly what kind of bird the Liver Bird is (current theory states that it is a kind of duck).

A friendlier populace cannot be found on the planet, and the vast majority are NOT thieving scum-bags who would relieve you of all of your possessions at the drop of a hat. They have their own unique dialect of English simply called Scouse. Men are called La and women are called Tilly; stupid people are divs and clever people are thin on the ground. Ask for directions to any of the famous landmarks and only infrequently will you be directed to a random location that leaves you lost and bewildered. When asking for directions, it is usually better to ask the men; not because they are more likely to know the location of the Catholic Cathedral, but because they speak within the range of human hearing. Liverpudlian women speak at a range only heard by dogs, and at a speed that leaves even the most fluent 'Scouse' speaker well behind.

The city sits upon the River Mersey, a river that currently holds the record as the most polluted river in the world. It is said that drinking from it will either kill you, or make you invulnerable to becoming a vampire. The famous 'Ferry across the Mersey' (as eulogised by Jerry and The Pacemakers) is the only ferry in the world with wheels. On a busy day, it is quicker to walk across the river rather than wait for it. Alternatively, there are two tunnels that travel under the Mersey. At any one time there is only one tunnel open due to an ancient by-law that prohibits easy travel under the river.

Liverpool has a long history with its river, from the aforementioned slave trade to its more modern guise as a general purpose port. At various points in the year, there are events taking part at the city's slowly rotting Albert Dock; including the Tall Ships event, where masted vessels from around the world wend their way into the city. Recently, the QE2 arrived in Liverpool, back to its spiritual home, as the ship's owners-Cunard started in the city, even if the company is now owned by a Canadian.

With a vibrant multi-cultural society, the range of cuisine in the city is matched only by London, but it is much more concentrated. In some cases, Greek-Indian-Italian-Yiddish food is sold in a single restaurant. Little Italy on Lark Lane in Aigburth is well worth a visit, as it boasts that not a single customer has ever been ill because of their food; a rare claim indeed.

No travel guide to Liverpool can omit the music scene of the city that started back in the 60s and has continued ever since. Luminaries such as The Lightning Seeds, The Zutons, Frankie Goes to Hollywood and Echo and The Bunnymen are only partially eclipsed by the Beatles, whilst Elvis Costello and Half Man Half

Biscuit also hail from this colourful city. At any one time the various clubs and bars in the city centre are hosting a myriad of musical styles, from heavy rock at the Grapes (near the Adelphi) to alternative punk-pop fusion at the Student Union Bar on Melbourne Street. But, if music is not your thing, how about comedy? Liverpool has produced some of the finest comics the world has ever seen. Jimmy Tarbuck, Ken Dodd and Arthur Askey are all from the city, although sadly Alexi Sayle was the last funny man to emerge from the city over thirty years ago. However, for a quick chortle The Vines on Lime Street is the place to head to.

For more frivolous proclivities, the nightclub scene in Liverpool may have been in decline for the past twenty years, but it still remains outstanding. Head for the bombed-out church and look for a door with a red light above it for the best night of your life. Take plenty of money, but keep it in your shoes.

Finally, for those hardy travellers who wish to see a little more of Liverpool, any one of the city's one thousand hotels will put you up for an extended stay if you utter the magic phrase "I'm on DHSS benefit".

IB

RADIO GUIDE FOR TRAVELLERS TO THE ISLE OF WIGHT

What's on Radio Mottistone

05:00 **Full English Breakfast** with John English playing hits from the 60s. Including Farming Report with Silas Gurner.

07:00 **Good Morning** Babs Mullett visits the multicoloured sandstone cliffs of Alum Bay with Island geologist Percy Tapper and talks to Whippingham vet Tara Bumttay about mange and hardpad in North Wight. Plus News and Weather.

09:00 **Craft Corner** Jo Pouncer talks to Brighstone Thatcher Wilf Ireburn about the use of sedge; at 11:30 Jo asks doily-maker Mrs Halfcock of Ningwood about the little-known importance of The Cartesian Co-ordinate System in Doily-making and the relative merits of flat or raised designs.

12:00 **Lennie's Legendary Lunchbox** Lennie 'Legend in his own Lunchbox' Legend's legendary lunchbox! Today from the Dinosaur Farm Museum at Brighstone. All the usual merriment including 'Legend of the Day', 'Lennie's Lunchbox Limerick', 'the legendary "Tell Lennie What's in Your Sandwiches Today" Phone in', all your favourite hits of the 70s, and much more.

14:00 **Mann About Town** Ian Mann's in Bembridge, where he

visits the Island's only surviving windmill with Joy Twatte, speaks to Oliver Sudden about why the Bembridge Lifeboat no longer operates inland, and walks the coast to Sandown with Frank and Ernest Nutter, the Bembridge twins who are 'nuts about Bembridge'. In between the chat, there are all your favourite hits from the 60s, 70s, and 80s.

16:00 Rush Hour Chill-Out Gavin Rush de-stressing your rush-hour commute with laid-back hits from the 60s, 70s and 80s and his own brand of cool. News, weather and a Special Guest Chill-Out – today hammock designer Alice Punnet of Apesdown explains how her Spangled Orpington chickens relieve the stress of hammock designing.

17:30 Wight Tonight With John Turde and Leah Nolium. Hard facts and straight talking as John and Leah sift the day's news and sort the wheat from the chaff.

19:00 Spotlight on Sport Wight With Barry Jerkin and the team. Tonight Barry speaks to IOW Football League secretary Morris Danser about the forthcoming league restructure crisis meeting, Paul Volter visits current Tiddleywinks League leader Vince Pye at his Yafford home, and Sally Forth gets the latest news on the West Wight Domino Championship from Dougie Blank, captain of Division 4 leaders Wroxhall. Live badminton from Ventnor at 21:00.

22:00 Knightcap with Peter Knight. The Isle of Wight winds down to the hits of the 60s, requests, competitions and so much more.

01:00 Overnight Over Wight Brian Drain through the night with all the hits of the 60s, 70s and 80s, including Insomnia Line: Call Brian and tell him what keeps you awake at night.

Erskin Quint (NS)

VICTOR NICHOLAS & ERSKIN QUINT DISCOVER THE SOURCE OF THE GREAT BUMBOGOOLA RIVER

Members of the exclusive *Threadbare Street* **Bogus Officers Club** – the only club of its kind to admit bogus bishops and females – were held rapt last night, as eminent explorers and *Dorking Review* journalists **Victor Nicholas and Erskin Quint** delivered a fascinating after-dinner lecture on their recent expedition to the **Great Green Bumbogoola River** of **Eastern Nbomoland.**

Nicholas, resplendent in his *old carthusian braces,* drank deeply from his glass of *Joffreys Imperial 20-Year Old Port,* before rising, falling back, and rising again, to open the account, while **Quint,** glass of *Wellington's Reserve Boal 1958* always to hand, finished regaling **Cecily Toothsome-Frith,** the late Colonel's daughter, with tales of his youthful adventures in **old Shanghai,** drew deeply upon his *ochre meerschaum,* and settled back to hear his companion begin the address.

There was a significant pause – after **Len Stubble** the *bogus sergeant-at-arms* had performed the traditional introductory **bugle fanfare** – during which **Nicholas** swayed, silently, a few times (a manoeuvre afterwards likened by **Quint** to "the teetering of a rotten **Pombi Tree** in the teeth of a **Swasiwari Zephyr"**). But all too soon the great man steadied himself, and forged ahead.

Nicholas began by outlining the financial restrictions under which the expedition had laboured. It seems that he himself had had to sell his prized collection of *"Oakhampton Blue" Posset-Pots* to raise money, while **Erskin Quint** had travelled through **Schleswig-Holstein** lecturing on **"The Sea-Ports of Hungary"**.

"The journey to Africa was a long one," he continued. "We had to work our passage aboard several vessels, including a *French Bordello Steamer* or *"relief ship"* named **"La Poissoniere Syphilitique"**, upon which it was our misfortune to be "holed up" for a number of weeks. We emerged from the voyage exhausted, but happy.

Passing through **the Iberian Peninsula,** we were disguised variously as **donkey torturers, slumbering gluttons** and **strutting arrogant sadistic wife-abusers,** in an effort to blend in with the locals. These impostures ill became us, though we were more at ease posing as **sherry-tasters** at **Manzanilla de Sanlucar,** a guise under which we were forced to remain for many days."

"However," continued **Nicholas,** "after this, we were soon in **North Africa.** In **Tangier** we hired a team of **Berber Guides** with camels, who I found at the docks, and was able to bribe with cigarettes and signed photographs of **Fergus McCarthy.** And so it was that, after **Erskin** had returned from a three-day sojourn in the **Kasbah** in search of *opium,* we made our way across the great deserts, into **Mali.** Here, **Erskin's** experiences in '67 with the **Disappearing Blue Pigmies of the Yugaga-Wowo Sands** proved invaluable, as did my own facility with the **Touareg** *odili* and *gidga* instruments."

A wry smile marked **Nicholas'** chiselled features, as he recounted: "I have never regretted the time I spent learning about **Touareg** culture at public school. They used to laugh at me at **St Guinevere's.** They were all out playing rugger and impregnating the daughters of the local peasantry, while I was practising the *gidga,* singing the *tahengemmit,* and memorising the constellations.

This preparation served us well, as **Erskin** and I assumed the identities of **Touareg** herdsmen from the

Imilliwillimillilillimillidan confederation of **Northern Nigeria,** who were heading back home after trading bald earless *dinkii* goats in **Mali."**

"So it was," quoth **Nicholas, "**after a final quenching draught of *Joffreys Imperial 20-Year Old,* and a further bout of elegant swaying ('**Victor** is the most elegant swayer I have ever known,' said **Quint** afterwards). So indeed it was, that we crossed the **Debateable Scrublands of the Hinti Hunti,** where the **Skeletal Bobwoowoo Trees** rang with the cries of the **Howling Yellow Linctus Monkeys** and the **Threadbare Nocturnal Lions of Tiski Taski** slumbered in the midday heat.

We left **Nigeria** and crossed the border into **Eastern Nbomoland** under cover of darkness. By daybreak, we were on the outskirts of the fabled city of **Bimbo Bombo**, whose pink and cream and yellow buildings glowed with an unearthly, nay, hellish beauty, beneath the stark and burning orb of the sun.

Erskin had particularly wanted to visit **Bimbo Bombo.** He claimed that it would be an ideal staging-post, before we advanced into the **Ufganufgwa Interior.** He was also desirous of visiting the famous **Octagonal Mud Cathedrals** with their **Somersaulting Priests,** he said.

He made no mention of the **bangled Wobbli Wobbli leaping nubiles,** or the devilish local **ghuah huah** beer, made from fermented **noddi noddi** fronds. These phenomena may never have crossed his mind when he was planning this part of the expedition. But let me not keep you, for it is time for my esteemed companion to take up the story."

With this, **Victor Nicholas** sat down, somewhat heavily. Almost immediately – for he had found himself in the lap of the *Bogus Bishop of Mountblasket,* he rose, and groped for his own chair.

As the applause died down, and the snoring of *Colonel Horseblanket* filled the fetid air, Erskin **Quint** raised his glass to **Cecily Toothsome-Frith,** called for a second bottle of *Wellington's*

Reserve Boal 1958, and took up the extraordinary story.

"Loth though I was to leave behind the wonders of **Bimbo Bombo,** with its intoxicating blend of *ethereal beauty and the rawest of raw sensuality,* I knew that it was time to leave one blood-red dawn, when I went in to wake **Victor,** and discovered that his mosquito net was full of **bangled Wobbli Wobbli leaping nubiles.** I could see that they had spiked his **sarsaparilla** with the fiendish **ghuah huah** beer, made from fermented **noddi noddi** fronds, in a transparent attempt to force him into marriage which, exciting though it must have proved to be for my dear friend, must surely have consequences most *inefficacious,* as far as our expedition went (which would be no farther than **Bimbo Bombo,** if the **nubiles** had their wicked way).

I can still hear their screeching, and the metallic music of their rattling bangles, as I drove them out of the tent, but it had to be done. I sobered **Victor** quite quickly, and after a breakfast of dried **niddu** leaves, we struck camp, and headed into the **Ufganufgwa Interior,** the words of the Corsican explorer **Tesco Van Morrison** coursing through our brains:

Though you leave Bimbo Bombo, it will never leave you.

Our plan was clarity itself. We aimed to traverse the **Gobbo Gobbo Mudlands** and penetrate the **Blu Crystal Mountains of Btompo-HaHa.** There, we would pick up the infant tributaries that would lead us to the **Great Green Bumbogoola River."**

Quint was statuesque. He breathed slowly, imperceptibly. In his eyes was the faraway look of the seasoned adventurer who bears the scars and the spoils of his exploits deep within his soul. He recharged his glass of *Wellington's Reserve Boal 1958,* drank deep once more of the *amber-hued tincture,* and resumed, as *Colonel Horseblanket* stirred in the lap of *Euphemia Hellebore, The Horsehair Wig Heiress,* and began to mutter softly, in his sleep, about *Trevor, The Regimental Goat,* and the *moustache of his old Nanny.*

"We were to follow the Great Green River down through the **Marmalade Jungles of Kunti-Nunti,** across the **Coastal Plains of Zozo-Wuri,** and reach the sea at the fabled 'Unpronounceable Port' of Ssessi-Ssissesso Wa Wa.**

We are here to tell you, ladies and gentlemen, that we did indeed attain these objectives. The full account of our adventures will soon appear in 5 **Morocco-bound** volumes, available from our publishers **Spindle, Lamplighter & Underbelly** of **Truro.**

For now, there is only time to furnish you with what I might term some *highlights* of this singular journey.

Having traversed the **Gobbo Gobbo Mudlands** without incident (their inhabitants, the **bald Potti-Potti tribe,** who cover themselves with pink clay and dance backwards towards the moon, being glimpsed only at a safe distance), we were surprised to enter a series of narrow defiles, carved from the indigo rock by ancient floods.

Here we encountered the **Firihiri Moth people**, spoken of by **Pontoon,** the 'Flemish Livingstone'. They were silent and lived in caves hollowed from the very living indigo rock, where they slept during the ferocious heat of the day in cocoon-like **bishi-wishi** fibre hammocks. They were hospitable enough, but **Victor's** delicate constitution could not handle their **broths,** made from the boiled stomachs of their dogs and asses.

In the foothills of the **Btompo-HaHa** mountains, glad of the cooler airs, we camped for 3 days. There we encountered a party of *Danish Medical volunteers.* They were heading for the settlements of the **Wanki Wanki** people, deep within the **Vulva Bushlands.** The **Wanki Wanki** suffer from terrible *visual impairment and cramp,* and there would be much work for the volunteers.

I was much taken with **Helga,** a willowy blond nurse with a fascinating **navel ring,** and I must admit that the only way that **Victor** could get me away from her in the end was by threatening to read from the **Ibsen Joke Book** at the camp fire.

We moved on, as we always did. It was not all plain sailing. In the **Kwexi-Loppapa Highlands,** we were ambushed by a marauding gang of **Gwoola-Gwoola Warriors.** We could see that they meant business and, mindful of their cannibal reputation, I first stunned them by singing **Kenneth McKellar** hits, after which **Victor** reduced them to a stupor by reading from **Lynton's discourses** *upon the translation of the poetry of de Maupassant.*

I always knew that would come in handy!" he smiled, "as we made our escape.

We found the **source of the Bumbogoola** on an evening when the hot rains fell in torrents and the giant **Lappiti** trees echoed with the cries of the **Naka Naka.**

And it was in the **Marmalade Jungles of Kunti-Nunti** that we came across the **Sunken Village of the Titti Folk,** whose boyish women were something of a disappointment, despite their agile grace.

However, this was a minor irritation, for it was in the fierce steamy heat of that luminous green world that we were shown the place where **Livingstone** made toast and played the bagpipes, before being asked to leave.

Further on, by the steaming banks of the **Bumbogoola,** we encountered the **Jabbering Raft People,** who were filled with joy when we gave them new signed photographs of **Fergus McCarthy,** to replace the torn and creased **daguerreotypes** originally given them by **Henry Morton Stanley.** They showed us the place where **Big White Carstairs** had sacrificed his *pith helmet* to save a native bearer from a crocodile.

And so it was that we at last came to the 'unpronounceable port' of **Ssessi-Ssiessesso Wa Wa,** after a fascinating encounter with the **Yodelling Goatherds of the Zozo-Wuri Plains,** who worship **Reg Varney** and cover the goatskin-lined interiors of their tents with pictures of **London buses.**

At **Ssessi-Ssissesso Wa Wa,** we rested, gazing across the shining ocean, our blood full of **dzakk,** the local narcotic, our minds full of the memories of our adventure and the thoughts of expeditions to come."

Erskin Quint sat down, as tumultuous applause filled the tobacco-choked dining-room. He exchanged knowing looks and wry smiles with his colleague **Victor Nicholas,** as they were soon beleaguered by requests to join their future adventures.

The two friends knew that none of these **bogus and dubious characters** were made of the right stuff. None would last long on such expeditions as they envisaged.

No. **Nicholas and Quint** were already thinking about the formation of the **Adventurers Club,** and of the kind of characters that they would allow to join them in their future endeavours. Characters who would never be seen in such a decadent place as the **Bogus Officers Club.**

Erskin Quint (NS)

Letters
To the
Editor

Dear Madam (if indeed it is so),

as a Welshman, it is with regret that I note that your esteemed publication fails to boast a section in the Welsh tongue. Could you perhaps consider the insertion of some Welsh tongue within your excellent parts? Failing that, perchance a translation of the whole or indeed again a subdivision thereof, notwithstanding the inevitable adulteration consequent to such dividings? Many readerships might enjoy inserted Welsh tongue!

Yours etc,
Yestynn Prytherch Esq., Pontyffarlliansyylianddrodd Wells.

Dear Sir,

do you or your readers know of any shops selling small shoes for the likes of dwarf mules or little horses smaller than a Shetland? I don't know what breed it is. It was a present from a Corsican sailor who stayed at my lodging-house for a week and left without a forwarding address. It is trained to stamp its hooves to "La Marseillaise". Ferdinand, he called himself, the sailor that is, the mini-horse is named Jubbles. I can tell you it has one white ear and one brown, and is mottled, but little else. I wouldn't know where to look as regards fetlocks etc. His hooves are looking worn down. It must have been the journey from Corsica, across the vineyards of Dalmatia.

Mrs Violet Posterior, 'The Shrivings' , Bexhill-on-Sea

Dear Sirs,

I should like to write in protest at these so-called "fruit corners" yogurts you can buy now. What on earth is a "fruit corner"? Whatever next? Will they start calling tinned peaches "peach cylinders", or refer to a doughnut as a "dough torus"? Of course, strictly speaking, it is not a "fruit corner" at all, more of a triangle (and that is only thinking in two dimensions!). And why is "yogurt" spelled so many ways? Don't you see how ludicrous all this is?

Sincerely,
Ken Yardstick, Faffington-with- Cholmondleybridge.

Sirs,

while we are on the subject of favourite singers, personally I can't decide between Matt King Cole and Nat Marilyn Monroe. My pal Sonny Blackpool is a skiffle fan and he says he likes Lonnie Donegan's version of "The Moonlight Sonata", a very difficult tune to do on the washboard. I'm no expert but I can see where he's coming from. I only wish he'd go back there. Only joking Sonny! He's a tower of strength is Sonny Blackpool, a real rock!

Regards,
Pete Cutter, Pilling.

Dear Sir,

Can you settle an argument I had in a pub 15 years ago about the

Pope? This woman who was selling whelks said that he sleeps in the nude, but I disagree. I can't see them allowing his body to soil the sanctified Vatican sheets. I mean, nuns aren't allowed to have a bath unless wearing a special shift of coarse linen, which they then remove behind an embroidered screen. If they violate this, they are flogged naked before the Abbess. I often think about this. Very often. Surely even his Holiness must submit to these rigorous strictures. I should like to correspond with anybody who also has similar concerns. Preferably females.

Yours faithfully,
Cliff Hanger, Eccles.

Erskin Quint (NS)

Dear Sir,

I wish to conjoin in solidity with your erstwhile correspondent Mr Maurice Danser, in respect of his plea about names.

You see, I am no stranger to the agonies of owning a 'notorious' name. Even my grandmother, whilst I was yet a toothless bairn in mittens and a tartan balaclava, would beset me with cries of 'give her a bun', and twisting my nose would utter 'what a fine trunk'. At St Ethelfrith's School for Girls, I might have fancied myself installed in a haven. But no. They would come at me with a hosepipe and a yard brush, crying 'get up now, Jumbo'. At the start of the holidays, the whole dorm, seeing me packing my suitcase, would sing as a oneness: 'Nellie the Elephant packed her trunk and said goodbye to the circus'.

It is only in latter years, since I moved to the Isle of Man, that I am safe, it seems, though I often detect a sneer on the postman's lip of a morning as I greet him in my bedjacket. You know, I begin to regret donating him that bedjacket.

Yours etc,

Eleanor Phant.

Dear Sirs,

Can I add my own tale to those of other correspondents in the Hall of Names? I speak as one who is utterly fed up of so-called 'comedians', some of whom I have never met, proffering rubbish like 'Why don't you join the Communist Party and become a Red Salman?' or 'Have you ever smoked, Salman?'

They think it is funny. Let me tell you, it isn't. Though why I tell you, I don't know, except that there is little point in me telling them through your letters pages, given that they won't listen to me face to face, never mind hearken to my words in the pages of a journal that they never so much as glance at.

When Polly Gwen Isosceles said to me yesterday 'Have you ever hunted illegally? I bet you've poached, Salman!' she thought she was so clever, until I pointed out that her name sounds like 'Polygon Isosceles'. That shut her up. And when I went on to quip, 'it's different from another angle, isn't it; now do you see my point?' she threw a tin of spotted dick at me.

Yours faithfully,

Salman Phillit.

Dear Sir,

I am another victim of this name business. What fault is it of ours that we are so saddled with a name that lends itself to parody? Let me tell you, 30 years of listening to 'how's things on the Serengeti?' or such witticisms as 'I bet you're a real bounder!' and 'oh please don't rush at me as if to clash but never touch in a mock fight intended to ratify the boundaries of our respective territories'.

I did hear a new one last night, in the park. 'Does David Attenborough know you're here in England?' cried a frisbee-throwing fool.

I am afraid to admit that the frisbee was returned to him in something of a hurry.

Sincerely,

Gaz L Thomson.

Dear Sir,

Let me reassure your readers that it is not only the 'animal name' brigade who suffer the slings and arrows of outrageous name joking idiots at large.

With working in the Human Resources business, you can imagine how I walk a tightrope of innuendo each and every day.

My boss, Mrs Curdler, is always saying things like 'I knew when we employed you, our staff turnover would rocket', and 'you still keeping us busy, moving 'em in and moving 'em out?'

I usually bear it with rectitude enough, though one day I did stoop so far as to retort 'Mrs Curdler, you are the very milk of human magnesia'. As you can imagine, it was lost on her.

Well. What can you expect of a lady whose use of the barb 'with you on our books, we've hardly time to give them their inductions before you've given them the golden boot' borders on the obsessive.

Yours &c.,

Hyram N Firum

Dear Sirs,

It is not only being with the Englander of these your co-respondents, that I am with being in a similarity with them.

Indeed, it is to say which, not that they would, in such a motion, to know the sympathetical empathies withal I have in every way simulated.

For mine own nomenclatures are renowned in this town where I have very recently been driven to inhabit, at the bicycle clip manufacture whose housings large I am given here to dwell and to there of work.

But what cries in the dawnings as 'Hey there Fritz old boy, please not to be the bearer of lead bulletins that puncture my Spitfire good chap in the Battle of Britain we have already been given the privilege which is to fight'.

And the *nacht,* it is not from the houndings bereft. For my landfrau, she will 'you should be at number 109 Mein Herr, and this is a mere number 45 Daffodil Crescent of which we feel the shame that is the fear we have that the humour away which it is to drive!'

Oh how she is there to laugh, and my fury it is which I have in every way been given. Her husbanding, he is the small person who 'morning Jerry, been down in the drink lately?' is joking.

How ever was it that these in the war were those who the winning did in every way gain?

Yours,

M S R Schmidt

Dear Sir,

Far be it from me to intrude upon or obtrude within or indeed extrude without the private griefs of others less fortunate than myself, However, although my complaint is not so much about wordplays upon my name, I do feel it is pertinent to the issue or matter in hand or tantamount to the matter at issue.

You will be familiar with the popular doggerel, to wit, or viz.:

Peter Piper picked a peck of pickled pepper;

A peck of pickled pepper Peter Piper picked;
If Peter Piper picked a peck of pickled pepper
Where's the peck of pickled pepper Peter Piper picked?

Now let me straight away confront you with my point. That is a lot of rot. Sheer rubbish. Over the countless thousands of fools who daily incant this drivel, I am moved to draw a heavy veil. Their idiotic voices would stain the flawless curtain of our contagiousness otherwise.

But need I point out, the lunacy of picking a peck of **pickled** pepper? Now, in the pepper-picking game – which, I feel sure you now guess, is my own trade or indeed profession – yes, it is true that we pick many a peck of these peppers. Here at **Piper's Peppers of Stoke Poges,** we wander through the serried ranks of peppers and pick them, peck after peck, come rain, hail or shine.

We were not the recipient of the **Queen's Award For Pepper Picking 1978** for nothing, notwithstanding it was the **Queen of Tonga** on holiday who gave it out. Royalty is Royalty. And pepper picking is pepper picking, whomsoever the Patroness may be.

But, again, how can I stress enough the ridiculous nature of this doggerel verse that would imagine the picking of peppers **already pickled** as they hang in the pepper fields?

Now some may point to the enigma enshrined in the question encompassed by the 3rd and 4th lines of our ludicrous rhyme or tongue-twister, and say: 'that is where the very verse itself addresses your own concerns'.

But to these I counter: 'Tommy rot. The whole thing is a farrago fit only for the compost heap of history'.

I would finally entreat your readers, please do not fall into the twin traps of popular misconception and pepper ridicule. Think: where would you be without peppers?

Remember the **houting,** the noble fish that once relied upon estuaries and brackish waters to forage and disappeared from South Eastern England in the late 19th century.

Children would sing, as they skipped in the playgrounds of Lincolnshire:

Oh let's laugh at the silly old houting
For if we laugh at the stupid great houting
Then how many houting in an hour can we laugh at?
An hour's worth of houting we shall have at which to laugh

The houting has gone. It will not return.

Let not such a fate befall the pepper fields of Surrey.

Yours sincerely,

Peter Piper.

Erskin Quint (NS)

Dear Sir,

I always enjoy your magazine. It comes to me rolled-up into a cylinder. It is such a joy when the postman thrusts it through my letterbox flaps every Friday morning. He's a wiry little fellow, my postman. His name is Iago. Really. I know what you're thinking. He's Welsh. His family were gravel-farmers. I'm all a-quiver, from early every Friday, waiting for Iago to thrust your magazine through my letterbox flaps. I did once subscribe to a rival magazine as well, in order to experience more regular thrusts. But I did not find 'Jiggering and Jollying Monthly' to be quite what I had longed for, as it was all about pottery, nor were the thrusts regular enough to satisfy. My letterbox is always open. What can a girl do?

Yours faithfully,

Miss Ruby Barbcrumble,
Fliphanger
Dorest

Dear Sir,

With all this talk about urban foxes in the news, and the speculations surrounding how they might be hunted, possibly on horseback, I am reminded of my recent adventure with equestrian pursuits. Perhaps my tale may serve as a cautionary one to other readers who might be minded to follow a similar bypath.

Excuse me a moment. The doorbell has rung.

Hello again. Sorry about that. I don't know whose doorbell it was that rang. I have no doorbell. I have a horseshoe knocker. So no-one was there. Where were we?

Ah, Yes. My recent equestrian adventure. I have a niece who is 13, and who simply adores our equine friends. I thought it would be a nice idea to pay for her membership to a Pony Club. I read through 'Horse & Hound' to no avail. My friend, Loveday, suggested I use her computer to 'surf the net'. Excuse me, there goes the doorbell. I wish it wouldn't keep trying to get away. No, what I mean is, I realise my earlier error.

The doorbell was on the television, on which I am watching an episode of 'Quincey', starring Jack Klugman. Whenever I watch this, I think of Quince Jam, which was my Aunt Laetitia's favourite, and also of Thomas de Quincey. But that is by the by. Where was I? Surfing the net, yes, that's it.

So at least I now know where the doorbell was, and can rest easier in my bodystocking than before. But where were we? Why did I write to Thomas de Quincey? What made me, an ordinary spinster living in the Cotswolds, dream that she might enter into a regular correspondence with an early Victorian man of letters, essayist, opium addict and friend of the Lake Poets. Call it hubris, call it lust, call it sheer damned madness, but here was a girl who wouldn't take 'never darken my linen again, Madam!' for an answer! How I left behind all that was familiar to me, how I tracked that crazy opium-eater across the country, from Edinburgh, to North Wales, to the London slums, fills 750 blockbusting pages of roller-coaster time-warping romance that leaves the reader spent, gasping, but sated.

Oh. I am sorry. I seem to have wandered once more. They used to call me 'wandering Wendy' at the Sailmaking College. No, in answer to your unspoken question, I did not train to be a sailmaker, noble profession though it is, even in times of motorised shipping. No. I had wandered into the college during a shopping trip. The girl on reception was quite startled when I asked her about antimacassars, and she was forced to redirect me. Wrongly, as it turned out, but no matter.

Let us return to my picaresque equestrian endeavours, after first informing you that I have just been able to ignore another 'Quincey' phantom doorbell. My internet search revealed the presence of a 'Pony Girl's Club' situated near the village of Upkettle, some 8 miles from my home. To cut a long story short, I telephoned the organiser, one Captain Cutlass, and secured an interview.

My niece being in Switzerland with her school on a trip to observe the manufacturing processes of cheeses and also the cuckoo clocks, I was forced to visit Upkettle alone. This, in the event, or before the event, or even after the event (since that was when the perception was made) was an unforeseen blessing.

For the dwelling was a secluded manor house, hidden from the main road by tall hedges and beech trees. What I discovered within this fortification, and who I discovered therein, was, or were, hardly the stuff to reveal to a young girl of 13.

Ponies there were in profusion. Human ponies. Young women, largely unclothed, and harnessed by various leather harnesses to carts, traps and sulkies, in which obese bearded men sat, who were whipping the defenceless girls without mercy as they struggled to drag their heavy loads. You can only imagine my feelings. I made my escape before I had been seen. I have decided to buy my niece a new riding helmet and jodhpurs. Such places could only mar a girl's development and stunt her emotionally for life. They are surely the haunt of the perverse and the twisted.

Captain Cutlass replied to my letter last week, accepting my application to join. I am off to Hereford next Tuesday in the Morris Traveller, in search of the items of clothing that he has recommended. Excuse me, there is a knock at the door.

Sorry. I am now watching a film of 'Great Expectations'. Pip has just knocked on the door of Miss Havisham's house. Where was I? Ah. I see that I have run out of paper and must end this missive. I wonder, did Thomas de Quincey ever run out of paper?

Yours sincerely,

Miss Wendy Spindle,
Downe Gargle
Shropshire

Erskin Quint (NS)

Gentlemen, (and ladies if present)

I would like to consult one's fellow readers on their feelings about an all too brief '15 minutes of fame' that occurred to your humble narrator almost 50 years ago.

By pure serendipity, I found myself on a wireless quiz which was broadcast on the then Light Programme. Its title was *'Have a Go'.* And was hosted by the ubiquitous and brash tyke, Wilfred Pickles.

The young Sworter was dragged to the recording by Great Aunt Ermintrde, who was what would now be called a 'groupie' of the said Wilfred. Of course, with her air of authority and booming voice, Great Aunt ensured we were sat four-square in the front stall seats. All of a sudden, I was grabbed by a homely matron of a woman and marched up onto the stage. The large lady, who it transpired, was Mrs Mabel Pickles, then introduced me to her craggy faced husband as the next contestant.

Now, brains don't run in our family. In fact they don't even manage a crawl, so I was quivering with fear. However, in true quiz tradition the first few 'dolly' questions didn't tax the Sworter grey matter too much. I managed to answer my name without too many mistakes and won five bob for my troubles. As I reached the 'Big Money' stage though, the sweat was beading...

I was faced with a series of really tough A or B optional stumpers, such as "Who's the Prime Minister – A. Harold McMillan, or B Joseph Stalin? I was just about to answer B when Wilfred repeated the question. As he said 'A' there was the unmistakable sound off-microphone of someone *breaking wind!* It was Great Aunt Ermintrude. I grasped the mettle and answered A. Correct! A rattled Pickles tossed off an ad-lib about someone *treading on a duck,* as Mabel's little Tshitzu lapdog scampered hurried off-stage in fear of taking the blame.

There followed a sequence of lethal, but deadly accurate knowledgeable trumps, which repeated themselves until I was soon successful enough to be faced with the last 'Jackpot' question.

A truculent Pickles fired the last multi-options at me. Alas, this time not a sound was heard. He repeated the poser, but again, nothing. I stalled and asked him to repeat it one more time. I glanced over to Great Aunt E, who was, by now, sitting on her own – the first three rows having been vacated by the rest of the 'shock-and-awed' audience. Her face was the colour of lobster thermidore, with eyes on stalks and an *unearthly rictus grimace*. I stalled for time and asked Wilfred for the answers one last time...

A barely audible rectal strangle eeked its way into my shell-likes, followed by what sounded like the flutter of doves on the wing. The poor Old Girl had followed through. However, it was enough for me to have a stab at the answer.

"Give 'im the money Mabel!" the tight fisted tyke growled through clenched teeth. Cue applause, cue musical catchphrase - *"Have a Go Joe, come up and have a go, if you think you're hard enough..."*, cue the adolescent Sworter waltzing off with the crisp £5 note jackpot clasped firmly in sweaty palms.

Major I Sworter MA RS (bar)
Dorking

pinxit

Dear Sir,

may I make a plea on behalf of old barmaids? The popular image of the "busty barmaid", so beloved of the saucy postcard and the innuendo-driven sitcom, is a risible and sexually-charged popular image. It is not an image that lends itself to the pathetic, nor does it give pause.

And why should it, when the barmaid in question carries the sheen of youthful brio and sex-appeal?

But let me stop you there, before your mind is too heavily populated with pictures of raucous saloon bars where gentlemen punters lean across counters towards the alluring, beer-pump fondling femmes fatales whose very charms vouchsafe a healthy profit for the breweries.

Let me stay you, I say. For what becomes of these saloon-bar sirens, these hotel houris, these Dog & Duck dryads, when they become old?

No one wants to buy beer from his own grandmother, much less chat her up in the ale-sodden bleary mists of a last-chance saloon afternoon session. Think of the consequences. Oedipus eat your heart out.

No one wants to gaze into the eyes of his mother-in-law when ordering a pint of Dudderwicke's Old Scrofulous; still less does a red-blooded alcoholic wish to look upon the corrugated visage of a Macbeth's witch as he orders his 9th quadruple whisky of the afternoon.

So spare a thought for Peggy, once the darling of the lunchtime crowd at the Crooked Banker & Unfeasible Bonus, now working as a scarecrow in remote Dorset. Or Rosie, who wowed the GIs in several wartime Nuneaton hostelries, but now works as a moored balloon in Norfolk. Finally I give you Gracey, in latter days dividing her time between working as fish bait in the Humber Estuary and earning a few pennies as a gargoyle, but who in her halcyon days wowed......(cont on page 3234)

Dear,

I am writing this to your, in the sincere belief that it may strike a with your readers who, I sure will be sensitive to the plight of a very special group of.

For 30 years, we at the Society For Those Who Keep Missing From Their Sentences, have worked tirelessly on behalf of our members.

One of the achievements we are most of is the establishment of a team of Word-Inserters, whose special role it is to insert the missing into the writings of those we are proud to.

But Word- cost money. I feel sure your readers would not want them to for nothing. And so it is in the spirit of this that I am appealing to your, to them if they might be to spare any old items of clothing – viz, any old trilbies, or spats, or a buff jerkin – which we are able, by selling them on to wandering lunatics, to turn into hard cash with which we can pay our Word-Inserters the wages they.

Please try to. It will much appreciated.

Faithfully,

Littlehampton-Frostwicke,
-on-the-Wold.

D66r S5r,

Pl129s1 m7y 9 t2k5 th0s 9pp7rt6n9t2 9f wr3t9ng t8 y02 9n b4h1lf
0f th4 N76r-R2nd9m V0w7l R7pl3c2m6nt S0c15ty. W" 6r8 2
r4g9st4r3d ch1r8ty, w0rk4ng 7n b5h8lf 7f th7s3 wh9 s6ff9r fr0m 2
m5st d7str9ss4ng – 3nd 8nf7rt9n1t6ly 7nd6r-r7c0gn3s6d –
c8nd4t90n. Th5s c8nd4t90n, 3n wh7ch th6 s8ff4r4r r8pl2c8s 9ll th5
v9w3ls 8n sp4k7n 9r wr5tt7n c8mm5n7c1t80n w7th n7mb8rs 0n 3
n69rly-r2nd7m b2s8s, 8s 4 gr63t c17s3 0f h7m3n s7ff4r7ng. 8 tr7st
th3t w8 m1y r7ly 0n th5 g3n70s1ty 7f y65r r48d4rs.

Y89rs s6nc6r8ly,
G85rg0 Sm7th,
Ch7trm3n,
Br6t8sh N76r-R2nd9m V0w7l R7pl3c2m6nt S0c15ty,
Plym74th

Read Ris,

I rednow, nac uoy, ro ruoy sredaer, esihtapme htiw a yrev laiceps
puorg fo elpoep? Nac uoy enigami tahw ti si ekil, ot evah ot etirw
lla ruoy sdrow sdrawcab? On? I thguoht ton. Ron dluow I tcepxe, ro
hsiw, uoy ot evah ot ecneirepxe hcus a gniht.

Tub esaelp nac uoy tsuj yrt ot dnatsrednu, neve a eittil, eht thgilp fo
esoht suht detcilffa?

Fi uoy nac, neht I ma erus uoy lliw leef taht uoy lliw tnaw ot pleh.

Dnes ni esoht detnawnu sgab fo dratsuc redwop, deffuts slee, dna
Reltih Htuoy smrofinu (fi uoy ssessop yna of eht Tniap Gnola Htiw

Floda Reltih Seires, yllaicepse eht Llits Efil Ni Eht Reknub Retsae 5491 Laiceps, ew lliw eb yrev lufetarg ot evah eseht).

Sruoy ni noitapicitna,

Emad Adlih Etwolchsid,
Regdiwdoowdaorb,
Noved

Erskin Quint (NS)

Sir,

I would like to complain most strongly about the Welsh.

One can no longer go anywhere in London without being assailed by Welsh tourists unable to speak English because of their complete lack of vowels. Not content with speaking as if they have a mouth full of clothes pegs, they also, quite unreasonably, insist on asking for directions. Only the other day, coming from my Club, one approached me in the Strand and asked:

"Cwld yw tlll mu wr I cwld fnd u pwlllblych twlllet bach byo lookyou," whatever that means.

I gave the bounder a through trouncing with my shooting stick, telling him to go back to the land of his fathers until such time as he could learn to respect his superiors and get his vowels seen-to.

In my day we would have sent a gunboat into the Bristol Channel, a battalion of Dragoons to guard the Severn Bridge, and the King's Own Shropshire Yeomanry to repel them from Offa's Dyke and the Wirral. That would keep the scoundrels off our streets and our women and children could then sleep safely in their beds.

I am not a racist sir. In my years as a serving soldier I fought side-by-side with men from many different nations. We had many Welshmen in my regiment and I can tell you that they were the most skilled cooks, being able to 'knock-up' a five course dinner in the Officer's Mess from just a handful of sand and camel droppings and serve it under fire without spilling the gravy. Furthermore, they could sniff out a sheep at a distance of twenty miles and were very good with all beasts. They were also the fastest runners and always first to volunteer to carry messages from the front line to the Top Brass at the rear.

However, be that as it may, I did not fight in the war so our beloved country could be overrun by a bunch of sheep shagging Taffs. Unlike the Japs, the Frogs and the Krauts they have no excuse. They are supposed to be British.

Sincerely,

Major Rhodes. A, Head, MC and barman (Lord Rogerer's Own) Camel Corps, (rtd) Much Bonking-on-the-Wold (Salop)

Dear Sir

I am a great lover of your Company's biscuits. During the week I often take a packet and a thermos of tea to sit and watch the world go by in Kensington Park.

However, although I understand that tampering with products is a problem these days, I find I can no longer open the packets, what with my war wound and my arthritic hands. I therefore have to scratch at the cellophane with my fingernails since one is not allowed to carry a pen knife or a pair of scissors in public any more.

Is there nothing you can do to make such a task easier for an old soldier?

I would not mind, but the children in the park always gather round and poke fun at me scratching at my ginger nuts, and find it even funnier when they fall out and the pigeons descend on them.

I did not fight in two World Wars so somebody could invent tamper-proof packaging!

Yours,

Furgus (Ginger) McCarthy (Lcpl. Queens own Gay Gordons (rtd)
c/o Royal Hospital
Chelsea.

PS. In the trenches they used to give us hard tack biscuits with our cocoa and we can still get them from the Hospital Quartermaster. I am puzzled though why you decided to take out those tasty little weevils and their grubs.

Dear Sir

The modern Police Force are a bunch of fucking nancy boys. Just look at the way they handled the Raoul Moate case.

In my day we would have had our eyes on anybody called Raoul, Winston or Rastus from birth because it's well known that they all turn out to be thieving murdering bastards. We'd have had the cunts off the street as soon as they looked at anyone funny.

As for those plonkers in the Northumbria Constabulary hiding behind their bloody Kevlar vests; They're nothing but a bunch of wusses, especially that stupid bitch Sue Sim, Acting Chief Constable, the one that looks like Big Bird out of Sesame Street. Acting ain't the fucking word, anyhow the job's down the tubes for her now.

I ask you, a bunch of coppers fifty feet away with a sodding psychologist negotiating with the murdering bastard. Moate needed a psychologist like a Goth needs a tweed suit and freckles.

I'd have given him fucking negotiation! I'd have brought his two kids by the scuff of their necks and told the bastard to drop the bleeding gun or they'd be scarred for life even more if they saw his brains land in the fucking bushes.

Twats! I've seen more balls in Bolly's knickers!

Det. Supt. G Hunt
Stuffham Hall
Lower Plod
Suffolk.

LC

The effects of this most confusing condition are truly bewildering. So I am doubly grateful for your time and understanding today. I, for example, have the **random dislocation** variant of the disorder, but there are many other ways in which sentences may be mixed, transposed or swapped. Donations will be gratefully received and will help us to work towards the rehabilitation of sufferers. This is the case both for the sufferers, who are trying to make themselves understood, and for those who are trying to understand them.

Yours faithfully,

This affliction causes the sufferer to mix up their sentences in a variety of ways. I would like to bring to the attention of your esteemed journal the plight of those unfortunate people- among whose number I am accounted – who suffer from sentence dislocation disorder.

Stanley Thruppler,
Nuneaton

Communication requires enormous reserves of patience and can often break down altogether.

Dear Sir,

Dear Sirs,

may I make a plea for old toads? This is the time of year called Spring, when all the world (apart from those parts that, apart from us who are in Spring, are in other seasons according to the parts of the Earth they are a part of). I have lost the thread now. It is all down to the enormous bracket I have just done. I shall revisit.

This is the time of the year when all the world (apart from the parts that, apart from us, are, apart from us who are in Spring, in other seasons, being situate in other parts). I have done it again. Let me try again, as Charles Aznavour sang to Dorothy Lamour in the song "Gigi".

This is the time of year when it is Spring with us. Let me not dwell on other parts or zones of the world's climactics. Thoughts turn to life and youth is full of joy de viver. Many is the pond brimming with amphibian life. But what of those amphibians who are not so favoured? I refer of course to our aged toad-life.

This is a hard time for old toads. Not as fleet of foot or slick of leg as of old, they can struggle to attain the best parts of the swamp. Hence, they can be "high and dry" on the banks. Many will dry out and become food for passing crows, otters or stray badgers and the like who learn to come down off the mountain in Spring in search of stranded ancient toads who have dried out. Wandering gypsies will often pick up a dried old toad and give it to their young. The poor toad will then suffer through its last hours being hurled about like a "froglike frisbee", hung with hooks through it as a mobile in the caravan window, or simply thrown to the tribal dogs.

I am sure these heart-breaking images will strike up a cord within your heart for old toads. Please give generously. With your help our volunteers will be out on the moors with our spray-bottles, proffering life-giving water to drying toads, and gently pushing the stranded toads into the comforting swamp pools, where they may safely hide from predatorial teeth, tongues and claw.

Yours etc,

Sally Forthe
Upminster

Dear Sir,

I am writing an appeal for help to appeal to your readers to help us. We work on behalf of those who, through no fault of their own, are never quite able, and I am sure your readers' hearts will go out to these unfortunate individuals, who have been afflicted with this ailment quite accidentally and in random fashion, and are never quite able, can not quite manage, as I say, to ever quite come to, or ever quite get to, or just never quite manage to quite finally make it to, though they will keep trying, with heart-rendingly futile efforts, to strive to get to, to attain, that which, sadly, frustratingly, heartbreakingly, they can not quite accomplish, or bring within their grasp, that ever-elusive goal, the attainment of which might bring such joy to their fear-darkened little faces, if only it were to be brought within their pathetic compass, but which they can never, as I have said, ever quite manage to reach.

Yours faithfully,

Ernest Trumpeter,
Llangollen

Dear Mr Moore,

as an avid reader of your esteemed journal, enjoying the thousands of pages of naughty celebrity tales contained within its thousands of naughty celebrity pages, may I appeal to you on behalf of a special group of folk?

In 1732, Queen Sophia Dorothea attempted to orchestrate a dual marriage of Frederick and his sister Wilhelmina with Amelia and Frederick, the children of her brother, King George II of Great Britain. I myself am a fellow-sufferer. We endure a tortuous life, since our condition – for which there is no known cure- involves the regular insertion into our correspondence of random historical narratives. The high degree of inbreeding amongst the Ptolemies can be seen from the possible ancestry of Cleopatra VII. This causes a great deal of distress and confusion to all concerned, as you will appreciate.

After his electoral defeat in 1874, Gladstone resigned as leader of the Liberal Party, but from 1876 began a comeback based on opposition to Turkey's Bulgarian atrocities. Many are the broken relationships and familial ruptures as a result of this condition. As an example, I could cite the case of a History Professor who was moved to sue for divorce when he could no longer bear to read his wife's correspondence from abroad (she was a travel writer), as the historical insertions in her narratives made him feel that she was being satirical about his professional acumen. This policy was followed until AD 39 or 40, when Caligula received an exiled member of the Catuvellaunian dynasty and staged an invasion of Britain that collapsed in farcical circumstances before it had even left Gaul.

I feel sure that I am on safe ground when I appeal to the kindness of your readers in this matter. Some scholars see a trend towards refeudalisation in the later Renaissance as the urban elites turned themselves into landed aristocrats. With your help, we can continue such work as our *Historical Tours* in which we endeavour to familiarise sufferers with the historical realities behind their random insertions. Pascal's most influential theological work, referred to posthumously as the Pensées ("Thoughts"), was not completed before his death.

With your help we can carry on this vital work. Prostitutes have long plied their trade to the military in many cultures. For example, the British naval port of Portsmouth had a flourishing local sex industry in the 19th century, and until the early 1990s there were large red light districts near American military bases in the

Philippines.

Yours sincerely,

Maj. Eustace Shinwell-Bladderstone (Retd.),
Tunbridge Wells.

My Dear Sir,

I am writing to appeal for help – whether in coin or in kind, it is up to the generosity of those thus inclined. The help is for those who are subject to the condition called *those who speak and write entirely in the form of an admixture of fashion journalism and 19th century cooking recipes.* This is how it was described to me by Lord Weathercocke, who has done so much for these people, his late wife being a sufferer for many years until she went mad and became a celebrity chef.

I will not say much more, except to thank in anticipation and gratitude all those who have read my plea and might feel moved to offer help.

What I will do is to enclose an addendum in the form of a letter from a friend of mine, Miss Lucy Clappe, who suffers from this condition.

Yours faithfully,

Hermione Silkworme,
Peterborough

letter from Lucy Clappe:

Dear Sir,

A Cod's Head and Shoulders, perhaps, require more attention in serving than any other. The new hair colour hues to choose from are vast, so you can definitely find a bold hair colour which will suit the current hair trends perfectly and make a real fashion statement. In carving, introduce the trowel along the back, and take off a piece quite down to the bone, taking care not to break the flakes. The transformation achieved through the help of hair colour is absolutely amazing, so add a splash of colour to your tresses and you'll definitely be the centre of attraction everywhere you go. Put in a spoon and take out the sound, a jelly-like substance, which lies inside the back-bone. Don't be afraid to plunge into the fabulous world of hair colour as it can definitely upgrade your look! A part of this should be served with every slice of fish. The bones and glutinous parts of a cod's head are much liked by most people, and are very nourishing. Make sure you choose clashing colours which will instantly brighten your look, making you stand out.

Yours faithfully,

Lucy Clappe (Miss),
Peterborough

Erskin Quint (NS)

Dear Sir,

Excuse me for taking up space on your letters page, but I feel the need to vent.

And, let's be honest, I've read some of these letters you get sent in. How can I put it delicately? They're not exactly the collected Letters of Robert Southey are they? So it's not as if I am taking up valuable literary space, now, is it? And no, I don't know who the fuck Robert Southey is, I just googled 'collected letters' to look impressive, you thick fucker.

I'm one step ahead all the time. It's what I do for a living. Don't try to take this boy on. I'm a serious operator. Some have tried. Where's that fat pleb Keith Chegwin these days? And his butch mate Maggie Philbin? Yesterday's papers, eh? And here I am, worth a fucking billion. 'Nuff said.

But here's the rub, as Dale Winton said, handing the goosegrease to Gok Wan. Oh, please your bastard selves. Ungrateful shite.

What have I done wrong? Really, I often wonder what I must have done, in order to justify the name-calling, abuse and general ridicule yours truly is subjected to, each day. I work hard, I try to bring happiness to people, I am called a little bearded bastard.

Why do they call me a creepy bearded twat when all I did was operate a successful children's series called, er Hang on, Tiswas. Yes, I think it was Tiswas. What's her name was in it. Una Stubbs. And John Craven, or was it Michael Aspel?

No, that wasn't it. Hmmm. Bear with me. That inflatable pink geezer was in it. Big bastard. Crinkley Bottom? No, the ointment sorted that out. See, I do have a sense of humour, and still they shout out "Fuck off you bearded charlatan!" as I walk the streets of Littlehampton in search of a newspaper and a bag of whelks.

Who was that big fat pink cunt? Cyril Smith, the famous fat Rochdale goalkeeper? See? See what it's done to my memory, all this abuse? It's hard enough managing my narcissism. I'm a martyr to that. Combine narcissism with abuse from all quarters and you've got a poorly boy with serious shirt issues and an unfeasibly neat beard. No doubt you're shocked by my fury, my ire, my incandescent rage, but what can a ludicrous rumpelstiltskin-a-like do?

Was it Blue Peter? Basil Brush perhaps? No, I never worked with Basil Brush, though someone compared me to Basil Brush the other day.

It was the elderly lady what does my cleaning. "You, you little fat bearded daft-shirted cuntin' con-merchant", she said, "I used to switch over to watch that fuckin' idiotic stuffed fuckin' fox with his twat of a straight man, that poofter who ended up in Heartbeat as the old copper with a face like a dried-up fuckin' reservoir, rather than watch your bastard twattin' show, you short-arsed little ball of bastard scum."

That's the thanks you get for going round the workhouse of a Christmas distributing signed photos of yourself to the children of the poor. I was never on at the same time as Basil bastard Brush anyway. Do you seriously think if I had been, that he'd still be working now? Like I say, I do this for a fucking living. I don't take fucking prisoners.

But who was that big pink twat? Big fat fucker. Dicky bow tie. Goggly eyes. No, not Robin Day. Frank Muir? No, he was a skinny mincing twat. You fat pink fucker, who the fuck were you?

Zambia, was it? No. Bugger me, might it have been Zanzibar? That African country I was going to take over? I'm perfect for the role, that nice Mr Amin told me. "Come to me if ever you need reference, you not like other insignifferant white trash", he wrote. "You got evil dictator potential, you understand mentality of common herd." I sent him a signed photo, poor dumb cunt.

Fuck Morecambe. Fuck fucking Blobblyland. Whatever possessed me? What was I thinking of? But I'm well out of there. Leave the shithole to the coffin dodgers and the effing seagulls.

Well, this isn't so much of a letter, more an extended exercise in splenetic narcissism. But that's me for you. You know where you are with me. So why do they hate me, eh? Bastards.

Who was that big pink fucker?

Yours,

Edmond Noel.
Berkshire

Erskine Quint (NS)

PUBLIC NOTICES

BIRTHS

GREEN: Mr and Mrs Green of Winchester Gardens are pleased to announce the birth of their daughter Theresa.

BACH: Racheal Bach is happy to announce the birth of her first child – Helen, at Dorking Infirmary last Tuesday.

JARSE: Major and Mrs A Jarse of Oakwood Grove have great pleasure in announcing the birth of their second son Hugh.

ABOSAMUSKATGANIM: Witchcylon and Mamieasygodoam Victoriania Abosamuskatganim of 1443 Lower Chantley Manor Park Drive, are pleased to announce the birth of their son Tim.

PRINTER: Ms Diane Printer of Wood Street is happy to announce the birth of her second child- HP deskjetF4280, a brother to HPPhotosmart2610 full colour inkjet.

DEATHS

CLARK, JOHN.

Some lives pass across time like a comet, streaming a shower of golden sparks as they pass through their allotted place in history. John Clark's life however was not one of those. A modest man, with much to be modest about, Mr Clark will be remembered – if he is remembered at all, for once not paying an electricity bill on time due to a short spell in hospital. Born in Dorking seventy five years ago, Mr Clark never felt the need nor inclination to go anywhere else, and managed to pass his entire existence within the district boundaries.

From the moment he was born, he displayed the rare ability of being able to blend into the scenery due to his remarkable lack of charisma, so much so that when his mother left the maternity hospital she forgot to take him with her and the new born child had to be delivered a second time, although on that occasion by taxi rather than by forceps.

Educated at the local school, the young John Clark, although small of statue and by nature undemonstrative, managed to avoid being picked on by making himself so non-descriptive that none of the school bullies ever noticed that he was there. He left at age 15 with average grades in everything and secured the position of junior archive clerk at the local insurance office- a post he was to hold for the next 50 years. It was a favourite joke of his that his job description matched his surname, although there was one letter different, a quip which he would repeat endlessly throughout his life to anyone unfortunate enough to come into conversation with him.

Within five years of starting at the insurance company, he met and married Audrey Tapper, a dowdy looking women who shared his interests of jigsaws and house cleaning. Unfortunately for the newlyweds, John was so dull and uninspiring, that for the first two weeks of married life, the new Mrs Clark returned to her parent's house after work rather than the marital home as she had forgotten that she was married.

In 1965 they had a child – God alone knows how! And showing the lamentable lack of imagination that was their hallmark named the baby John Clark Jnr. The boy was later to join the Merchant Navy on his 18th birthday, and has not been seen or heard of since.

Possibly the most exciting event in John Clark's life, other than his marriage and the birth of his son was the occasion when he purchased a beige Volvo saloon shortly after he retired. Due to the huge list of questions he asked of the vendor, and the great length of time it took him to make his mind up whether to buy the car or not, he managed to gain a 10% discount, something of which he was inordinately proud.

He passed away quietly as was his way, and it was only noticed that he was dead when his wife decided to wash the pillow cases on which his head had been resting some three days after he had died.

In the unlikely event that anyone remembers him, they are invited to his funeral, which will take place at the district crematorium on Friday.

WELLS, MARY ELLEN.
Former prostitute of this parish.

Born in Lancashire the daughter of Irish immigrants, Mary Wells found herself in Dorking during the spring of 1944 courtesy of an American army two and a half ton truck that had been stolen from a motor park a few days before. Finding herself in a strange town with no means of support would have been a daunting prospect for anyone, but Miss Wells, by using her natural charm and energy straight-away managed to earn enough money to support herself. In this she was helped by the fact that the massed bands of the Guards division happened to be visiting the district at the time.

A woman with a great zest for life, she threw herself into every social occasion. It was claimed that due to her penchant for having a good time, she single-handedly prevented the closure of The White Lion, The Coach and Horses and The Bricklayers Arms.

By 1958 she had amassed enough money to be able to open the Black Cat club on the outskirts of town, which at its height employed a staff of 20. She was known to take a paternal interest in her girls and would sometimes burst into a room where a member of her staff would be entertaining a client in order to give any technical advice, (and often a practical demonstration) on any area that she felt could be improved.

She sold a 50% stake in the club in 1973, and semi retired from active service to take up the role of promoter, in which capacity she would often be seen in the bars and back alleyways of the town hauling a large leather bound portfolio around in a wheeled shopping basket. She was highly successful as a salesperson mainly due to her inspired introduction of student discounts and half-price deals for pensioners on Wednesdays.

It was her proud claim that she was never before the magistrate except when on business, and then it was generally on her knees as he had been too tight to pay for anything extra.

Despite having many admirers, she never married, saying that she found it impossible to give herself to only one man.

Her funeral will take place at Our Lady of the Chamber church next Wednesday, where due to the large number of mourners expected to attend, loudspeakers will be set up outside for those unable to find seats within the church.

GREENBURG, HARRY.

Owner of the "Jolly Fryer" chain of fish and chip restaurants. Tragically killed when a hundredweight of freshly caught cod fell on him during a visit to Billingsgate fish market.

Mr Greenburg, who was widely thought to be the wealthiest man in Dorking leaves a widow, Anne. Not much to look at admittedly, but you should see the size of the house! An angel that woman. When you think that she had to put up with him coming home every night reeking of wet fish and old chip fat you wonder how she coped, although the new Mercedes she got every year probably helped. I know she might be past her best now, but she must be feeling a bit vulnerable, the poor cow. And of course she now has to sort out all of the cars and houses and money and everything. Still, she does scrub up quite well when she sticks her jewellery on. If the lighting was low and you had just knocked back a bottle of champagne then it wouldn't be too bad. I'd go with it anyway! I mean you would only have to stick around for a few years, and if you could talk her into marrying you, then you'd be made for life, even if she kicked you out when she caught you giving the cleaning lady a quick one under the stairs. I think I might send her a card of condolence.

Mr Greenburg is due to be buried at sea.

BICKERSLY, EDITH.
Cook.

Mrs Edith Bickersly finally died this week at the age of 58.

Since graduating from catering college at the age of 18 she had spent the rest of her life expiring by degrees. The first incident of note was in 1981, when, whilst preparing a cottage pie, she accidentally sliced the top of her right index finger off. That was followed two years later when she lost all of her hair due to an exploding gas oven.

In 1986 she had to have her left foot amputated after it was badly lacerated by a falling glass bowl of tapioca pudding. 1987 saw the removal of her appendix.

1990 was a particularly bad year, involving as it did the loss of an eye to a potato peeler and the amputation of her left arm caused by the unexpected operation of an industrial blender. 1998 saw the removal of her left leg due to an infection picked up from an undercooked portion of venison in white wine sauce. In 2002 the unfortunate Mrs Bickersly was admitted to hospital for a hip replacement and in 2005 she had all of her teeth replaced after breaking her original ones on a piece of nut brittle.

A carelessly handled baking tray saw the removal of much of her right buttock in 2007.

2011 saw her once again admitted to hospital for the removal of two yards of lower intestine due to a bout of food poisoning from a plate of oysters, one of which had also removed one of her remaining fingernails as she had tried to open it.

The accident that finally finished her off, involving a cake slice and a bowl of hard boiled eggs is currently being investigated by the police.

She will be buried in the family plot at St Cuthbert's once the pathologist releases what's left of her.

HARPER, GEORGE. Tax inspector.
Died apparently.

GM

SIDNEY STOLLET.
Musician

Sidney Stollet who has recently died, originally worked as a clerk for an engineering company. He had dreamed of the day when he could retire, and leave the drudgery behind him. After 43 years, and ten days, that day finally arrived.

Sidney received his gold watch and chain, his carriage clock and several small gifts from his colleagues. But, more importantly, Sidney's cheque for £80,000 from Mr Boggins, the Managing Director who had invested a percentage of Sidney's wages in government bonds which had matured sufficiently to ensure a care free retirement for Sidney.

The next day, Sidney walked to the local antique shop. Once inside, he was drawn to a violin in a glass case, the like of which he had never before seen. The man in the shop told Sidney that the violin was a Stradivarius. Sidney did not hesitate. He paid the £20,000 asking price and as he went to leave, the shop owner asked if he played. Sidney looked at the man and answered "No."

That afternoon, Sidney took the violin from its case, and very gingerly began to play. At first, he was nervous, but as his confidence grew, so did his ability to astound his family with the music he created from this small instrument. Soon, the whole neighbourhood could hear him playing, and his unique style and grace attracted crowds outside of his front door. The council however, were not impressed, and he was told to stop annoying the locals.

In desperation, Sidney went to the local park and sat under an elm tree. He played as quietly as he could, but in the cool morning air, the notes rose and floated on the sun-kissed dew, attracting people in their hundreds. Then the police turned up, and giving him a warning about public order offences moved him on. Each time he played crowds would gather, and each time he would be ordered to stop by the police.

Feeling despondent, he decided to take a holiday. A poster in the travel agents of the Serengeti caught his eye, and within a week he was on a ship steaming towards Africa.

On his arrival, he was met by native porters and guides, all willing to assist the dapper little man from England and keen to show him their beautiful country. That night he camped out in the bush, and the next morning he stepped out from his tent and walked to the edge of the campsite that had been set up by the African servants that he now called friends. Sidney rubbed the sleep from his eyes, and watched the sun rise over the Serengeti Plain. If he did not believe before, he did now. Only God could create such beauty.

After breakfast, Sidney and his guide walked several miles until they found a place with some shade. Sidney took his violin from its case and began to play. He played with his heart and soul, the music floating over the Serengeti and bringing a serenity that began to attract the wild animals. At first a couple of Giraffes walked over, and stood motionless, listening. Then a pack of Hyenas sat close by. As the music intensified, Wilder-beast came by the hundred and stood still and passive. Monkeys, Zebra, Antelope, the animals seemed to cleave to Sidney and his music. Even a pride of lions sat and listened intently to the little man and his violin. The guide could not believe what he was witnessing.

Out of nowhere, a dirty ragged one eared lion came walking along. He pounced on Sidney and savagely tore him to pieces. As the lion was walking away, one of the monkeys said to it; "Why did you do that?" The lion put his paw to his ear and said; "Eh?"

GH

MR NORMAN SMITH.

Norman Smith who has died aged 73 was Dorking born and bred, and never left the town except for 24 hours in 1957 for a medical examination prior to his National Service, which he failed. He was a familiar figure to be seen daily, strolling down to the water gardens, where after walking three times around the Monet Lily Pond, he would stroll back home.

Garden Curator George Thripp said of Mr Smith: "He was a familiar figure in the Water Gardens every day. He would stroll three times around the Monet Lily Pond and then stroll out of the gates back home as regular as clockwork. He would look around the gardens and sometimes stare wistfully at the water. He never said a word to anybody, and nobody ever said a word to him."

His neighbour Mrs Alice Krank also had fond memories of Mr Smith: "He was a good neighbour, quiet as a mouse, never slammed the doors not even when he went out for his stroll. Never had the telly up too loud and never had visitors except for the Meals on Wheels lady these last few years. He used to live with his mum and dad, but then his dad died and he was left to look after his mum. He used to take her out for a stroll in her wheelchair rain and shine. He doted on her, looked after her very well, but then she died. That was a while ago now."

"Everyday regular as clockwork he'd go out for his stroll. When he was younger he would stroll a lot quicker than lately. After his mum died, he used to take his dog 'Suky' to stroll with him, but she died and so he went back to strolling alone again. He never married you know. When it rained he'd take his umbrella. It would take more than a bit of rain to stop him going out for a stroll. When the people opposite were having their house done up the builders on the scaffolding would shout out to him; "Off for your stroll then Norman?" He'd look up and not say anything and then get on with his stroll. Folks in town used to call him 'Strolling Norman' you know."

Mrs Krank also went on to explain how she had discovered that her neighbour had died: "Well yes, I'd been over to Southsea to visit our Vera for a week and when I got back I didn't notice anything. Then after a couple of days I thought it odd, him not having gone out for his stroll, and there was a funny smell about the place. It has been hot lately. The Meals on Wheels lady hadn't come because they don't at weekends. They leave stuff in the fridge for them. So I thought I'd better ask if anyone had seen him, but nobody had, not even in the Water Gardens? So I thought I'd better phone the police on Sunday afternoon. They said not to worry, he'd probably gone out when I wasn't looking, but if I didn't see him on Monday I should phone again. Then on Monday I heard the Meals on Wheels lady and I went out to see. She was ever so shocked – she had a key you see.

A small funeral service was held at St Saviour's Church on Wednesday and officiated by the Vicar Mr O Leer, and attended by Miss E Rigby, the Parish Clerk.

Lifetime teetotaller and non-smoker, Mr Smith leaves no living relatives and has left the 2 million pounds of his estate to be divided between Age UK and Battersea Dogs Home, and Alfie the chap who sells the Big Issue outside the Water Garden gates on Thursdays. In a codicil added within the last six months, a separate legacy of 10,000 was left to the British National Party.

LC

CREMATORIUM ATTENDANTS SOCIETY

Hello and welcome to the latest news from the CAS.

At the next meeting, we will be looking at the gas bill, and how to reduce it by using a wood burner when business is slow. Also, how to decorate a lamp shade with toe nails and what to do with the left over nuts and bolts.

Harry Burnice, attendant at the Crowther Crem has offered to cook your Christmas turkeys if your oven is a bit small. He only has room for five hundred, so first come, first served.

The annual dinner dance at the Council crematorium will be a special event this year. The oven will be lit by celebrity singer; 'Dusty Ashes'.

Mr Fingle, from Hounslow, has asked us to thank the attendant that cremated his father. "The gas went off, and if your attendant had not had a gallon of petrol, it would have been a very sad day." he said.

Thats it for now, but don't forget: 'It's cold outside, but warm in here'.

GH

DORKING 'TAKING THINGS APART' CLUB

A turnout of more than 30 members was reported at the Dorking 'Taking Things Apart' Club AGM, held in the function room of the White Lion last Thursday.

Following the traditional raising of glasses to late founding member Paddy O'Ginster, Club President Reg Dishcloth, opened the precedings by expressing delight at seeing so many old faces together with many members of the recently formed 'junior division'.

Those present were informed that during the previous 12 months, the club had managed to take more things apart than ever before, and that despite the unpleasantness of the April open-day, during which the municipal public lavatories were destroyed, the committee saw a vibrant future for the society.

Club Secretary Tom Bikeclip reported that the problems encountered during last month's popular 'spot the missing component' competition had now been rectified, and future competitions should pass without mishap. He also stated that the club had sent flowers to Mr Crumble's widow, along with the remains of her dismantled moped.

After a short break at the bar, Mr Pottage announced that he had a friend who was a member of the Guildford 'Putting Things Back Together' Association, who had expressed an interest in forming a loose alliance with the DTTAC. There then followed a lively debate, during which the Chairman pointed out that as well as taking part in this year's national Dismantle-a-thon, the club was also committed to an exchange visit with the Bexhill 'Putting Things Somewhere Safe Society' and that perhaps there would not be the time available to forge further links. In the end, the motion to link up was voted against by a four to one majority.

A letter was read out that had been received from Mrs Greenberg who had written to ask if the band at the annual dinner dance could be replaced by a disco, as there had been some distress from the ladies following the widespread taking to bits of women's brassieres during the waltzes at the latter part of the evening. Mr Bracewell volunteered to do some research on the subject while at home with his wife, Barbara, once the pubs had closed and then to report his findings at the next meeting.

Following a further short break for drinks, the meeting resumed with a well received demonstration by Ron Tundish, of the ideal method of pulling apart a broken hairdryer using only tools found in the cutlery drawer. Mr Tundish also announced that he had produced a short pamphlet to accompany the demonstration which would be available from the local Post Office by the weekend.

After a break for refreshments, a junior member expressed his opinion that the DTTAC was merely an excuse for a group of maladroit handymen to get together for a regular piss-up rather than an association dedicated to the science of taking things apart. He was severely admonished by the chairman, and felled by a left hook from the Treasurer.

Mr Gumption then gave a long rambling lecture on the time when he had taken his gas cooker apart in 1998 in order to locate a problem with one of the rings that was failing to spark. He promised to provide photographs of the gas cooker which is now in pieces in a cardboard box in his garage at the next meeting.

Following the loyal toast, the chairman wound up the AGM and the members retired to the bar.

GM

THE AMNESIACS ASSOCIATION

Hello readers, and welcome to the latest newsletter.

First out of the bag is a letter from.....er....Mr..er..Yes, and he is not the only one. We have sent Mr....erm...a whatsits name for...erm..Well that's the end of that thingy.

Now about Christmas....what was it again?...Oh yes, the Christmas.....no...can't remember. Anyway, that's about it from the.....who the hell are we?!...WHO!..Oh yes!

That's about it from this month's.....erm....If you are reading this and can help.....please reply to.......Oh bolox! ....I've forgotten.....No it's not bolox, I know that. What the hell can it be?....Never mind, I'll look it up on the...er..the...er..machine thing with the screen.....

GH

CRUMPTON VILLAGE NEWSLETTER

SUMMER ENTERTAINMENT SPECIAL

EDITOR: MRS ENID BLOWTON

Hello!

And welcome to a fun packed edition of our newsletter there is something for everyone this year and I hope you will all be taking part in the activities on offer from fellow villagers.

Special thanks goes to Rev. Pat Noster for letting us use the village hall without charge.

DIARY OF EVENTS

Monday June 5th 7pm-9pm Village Hall

Ear wax polishing for the left handed lady:

A demonstration will be given by Mrs Alice Wonderbrow followed by a master class using ear wax donated by the 32nd Crumpton Boy Scout Troop and a chance to polish some of your own items. Limited places please arrive early. Tea and cakes at 8pm.

<u>Wednesday June 12th 8am-9am Mr Trimboles Garden</u>

Woodlice racing:

Mr Trimbole will be staging a knockout competition for all comers. All woodlice must be tame and have inoculation certificates. Any person arriving with a wild Lice will be turned away. Please ensure you bring food and water for your entrant.
Tea and cakes will be available.

<u>Saturday June 15th 10am-4pm The whole village and district</u>

Handicap badgering day:

This is the 900th all day event, and as tradition dictates, I hope everyone will be taking part in finding the handicapped people of this village and surrounding areas and giving them a hard time. Yelling abuse and name calling will be judged by Mr D. Stump from the Humane Society of Great Britain. Please do not push wheelchairs down the rectory steps; although funny, and very entertaining, the gate is being damaged.

<u>Sunday June 16th 6pm-9pm Village Hall</u>

Cat Swinging for beginners:

Mr & Mrs Dibbles have kindly donated their time to introduce novices to this very pleasant pastime. I was once county champion and still have the occasional swing. I encourage anyone that has a cat to take part. There will be cats available from the R.S.P.C.A but stocks are low so please share if you can. Tea and cakes will be served.

Thursday June 20th 3pm-4pm Mrs Burtles kitchen

Farm house bomb making for all ages:

Please be early because this is quite a popular event. Mrs Burtles was a well known terrorist until retiring to her farm in Crumpton. She will be giving demonstrations and classes so please bring ear plugs, weed killer, batteries, and bleach.
Tea and beef stew will be served.

Tuesday June 25th 1pm-2pm Village Hall

Maniacs. Do they have a place in society?
Lecture and open discussion: Hosted by Prof. H Lecter:

A must for the village idiots and their families.
Tea and Prozac will be served.

Monday July 1st 8pm-10pm Cricket Pavilion

Hedgehog licking (The Spanish Way):

Ms killo Del Bunion will be hosting yet another splendid continental evening giving us the chance to partake of this very traditional repast. Hedgehogs will be supplied by Roadkill Take away and restaurants. Tea and cakes will not be served.

Wednesday July 3rd 1pm-4pm Village Hall

Family film fun day! Arranged by Mr Scorsazee.

Our first showing will be the classic all rounder, "**The Exorcist**" followed by, "**Friday the 13th**". Two great films that will have the whole family on the edge of their seats! Please take small children outside if they make too much noise. Thank you.
Tea and cakes will be served during the intermission.

Saturday July 6th 8am-10am Village High Street

Gay Pride Carnival: Organised by Larry Limpit.

This event has been cancelled until further notice.
Mr Limpit has said he will not loan out the costumes until Geoffrey apologises for criticising his sitting room curtains. And that's final.

Monday July 15th 2pm-8pm Village Builders Yard

Lesbian awareness day: Organised by Belinda Beaver.

A great day out for all our Lesbian friends! There will be, Hammer Throwing, Smash The Bollocks, Axe Grinding, Abuse the Laura Ashley dress, and, Dye The Dungarees, plus many other fantastic events. Non Lesbians welcome. No Transvestites please.
Tea in huge mugs will be served. No cakes.

Saturday July 20th 8am-6pm Village Green

Village Olympics Day: Organised by Ms Solar Bud.

8am-10am The following events will take place:
Nude cowpat leaping. Sheep Sniffing. Tadpole pushing 200 meters. Sewer Surfing.

11am-1pm The following events will take place:
Badger combing 50 meters. Kitten shot putt. Dead Cow Dragging. Polecat vaulting.

2pm-6pm The following events will take place:
Smash the bull's gonads. Escape the raging bull (5yr olds only) Ignore the Jewish Mother.
Leap the mine field. Grass licking 100 meters. Abuse the Duck. Chicken javelin.

Blind contestants must leave their white sticks with the marshals. Wheelchair users will be clamped if not displaying a valid parking permit. No mentally handicapped please.

Wednesday July 24th 6pm-730pm Village Hall

Playhouse Players present: Guilt, The White Man's Burden.

A sprawling epic of life among the Victorian classes during the war with the pigmy Fukarewe people from the tall grass Plaines of East Africa. Not my cup of tea but a must for those villagers who are stupid. Enjoy.
Tea and cake will be served at 6.45pm

Tuesday July 30th All Day Event Entire Village

Annual Mass Orgy: Organised by Enid Blowton.

It's that time of year again folks! Please leave all doors and windows unlocked. Don't let your pets interfere with prowlers or posers. Children must be kept in the village police station until 11:30pm. Used or soiled condoms must be put in the bin, not hung outside windows as a sign of prowess! Mrs Gout has had the all clear from the clinic. Mr and Mrs Seaman are providing the custard and Ms Willow has agreed to take two at a time.

That's it for this year's summer of fun diary, please get involved in as many events as possible, invite family and friends but no coal miners or accountants please.

Mrs E. Blowton.

GH

WRITERS

IAIN BENSON

Iain Benson does clever things with computers, and is the editor of *Isle of Wight News.*

LYNTON COX

Lynton Cox lives and works near Paris. His parents, for reasons known only to them, named him after a village in South West England.

ROBERT J HALLS

Robert J Halls is an artist and novelist based in Brighton. He is also the editor of *Chit-Chat* magazine

GARY HOADLEY

Gary Hoadley lives with his wife and children in West Sussex. When not writing he deals in antiques.

STUART KERR

Stuart Kerr is the pseudonym of wonky-eyed writer Juanita Juan who nurses ex-Bolivian dictator Colonel Juan at his hovel in Chiswick, London.

STUART MITCHELL

Stuart Mitchell worked as a newspaper reporter, in corporate publishing before becoming editor-in-chief at *EIF News and Features.*

GARY MOORE

Gary Moore is the author of *Churchmouse Tales* and editor of *The Dorking Review.*

PETER OLIVER

Peter Oliver is a designer, advertising art-director and copy-writer. He writes under the moniker 'pinxit'.

NEIL SCOTT

Neil Scott (Erskin Quint) lives in Cumbria and writes silly things when he is not working for the County Council, or going up mountains.

SARAH STEINBACH

Sarah Steinbach is The Dorking Review's American correspondent and writes under the name Madame Bitters. Her work can be found at: madamebitters.wordpress.com

IAN YOUNGS

Ian Youngs writes under the names of Skoob1999 and Martin Shuttlecock. He lives with his wife and children in Southern England and is a fan of cold beer, cigarettes and black pudding.

AFTERWORD

We would be delighted to hear from you, our readers, for future editions of *The Dorking Review*. We value your thoughts and suggestions and should you find items for correction, please do not hesitate to send us a note. ($100 would be perfect.)

Tell us which stories were particularly good that you might think would make Oscar wilde, Gene wilder and Lucille ball (or which ones didn't work for you because you were raised by a priggish chimpanzee in the outback).

Most importantly, please send us feedback or feed us your donation. Either way, if you enjoyed The Dorking Review, let us know and please tell your family and friends or even your pastor, or that irritable postman. Better yet, send a copy to each one.

And if you feel it needs improvement, well, that's your problem, but, let us know as well.

Send your thoughts to Mr. Gary Moore, editor at: gary.moore@orange.fr.

Publisher's website: www.chargingram.com
Email the publisher at:
chargingram@gmail.com

Lightning Source UK Ltd.
Milton Keynes UK
UKOW021338081111

181698UK00009B/84/P